INTERNET RESOURCES

Job Seeking Information

- http://www.mnwfc.org
- http://www.jobsnd.com
- http://www.ajb.com
- http://careerlinknorth.com
- http://www.doer.state.mn.us
- http://www.usajobs.opm.gov/
- http://www.fedjobs.com/
- http://www.iwpr.org/
- http://www.ISEEK.ORG/
- http://excite.monster.com
- http://www.flipdog.com

Career Exploration

- http://www.mnworkforcecenter.org
- http://www.cdm.uwaterloo.ca/
- http://www.jobweb.org/catapult/Assess.htm

Table of Contents

FORWARD iii
INTRODUCTION v

1 TRANSITION
Change 1
Tips for Managing Feelings 10
Making Ends Meet 14

2 JOB SEARCH PREPARATION
Organization 21
Discover Where the Jobs Are 28

3 SKILLS IDENTIFICATION
Skills and Tasks 35
Goal Setting 38
The Employer Perspective 40
Addendum 41

4 RESUMES AND COVER LETTERS
Resume Formats 53
Resume Variations 54
Basic Principles of Resume Writing 57
Samples and Worksheets 63
Resume Strategies 73
Cover Letters 76

Table of Contents

5   JOB SEARCH TOOLS
- Employment Applications 85
- Reasons for Leaving 87
- Completing an Application 88

6   JOB SEARCH PROCESS
- How Do Employers Hire? 97
- Networking 100
- Direct Employer Contact 103
- Telephone Communications 104
- Personnel Staffing Services 108

7   INTERNET JOB SEARCH STRATEGIES
- The Internet Job Search 111
- Electronic Communications 115
- The Electronic Resume 117
- Hypertext Resume 121
- Internet Employment Service Providers 122

8   THE JOB INTERVIEW
- Interview Preparation 127
- Types of Interviews 130
- Interviewing Tips 132
- Key Interview Questions 134
- Legal Rights 138

9   FINISHING TOUCHES
- Thank You Letters and Notes 141
- Negotiating Tips 146
- Job Success Skills 148
- Conclusion 150

Foreword

NETWORKING—
The Golden Key of the Job Search Process

NETWORKING is a KEY CONCEPT to the job search process, from start to finish. Because of its importance, NETWORKING is briefly introduced here. The definition, explanations, and examples of NETWORKING are intertwined throughout the book. Special care has been taken to draw your attention to this concept whenever it is mentioned or implied. Look for the "key" symbol to help you identify it throughout the text.

The following are 10 important points regarding networking. Look for these points and how they can be applied throughout the job search process.

1. **Always Be Prepared**— Have business cards and copies of your resume with you at all times. Opportunities will arise anywhere and everywhere.

2. **Stay in Contact**— Keep your contacts informed about your efforts in the job search. They can be kept informed by short phone calls or brief handwritten notes. Be sure to send a thank you letter within 24 hours of an interview. Be consistent.

3. **Talk First with People You Know**— Talk to your friends, family, teachers, professors, former supervisors or managers, etc. Practice selling yourself first to those who know you.

4. **Contact People You Don't Know**— Begin contacting people to whom your friends and acquaintances have referred you. Initiate each conversation with information on how you received their name. Show an interest in what they have to say, not just what they offer.

5. **Ask for Information, Not a Job**— This is called an information interview. Detailed information is at the end of the chapter *Job Search Preparation*.

6. **Keep Conversations Focused**— Use each conversation to get good information. Give your contact a brief summary of your job search objective, major highlights, and accomplishments. Ask specific questions that will provide you with helpful insights.

7. **Look for Opportunities to Give Something Back**— Be prepared to offer something of value to those who are taking time to help you.

8. **Keep Your Promises**— When you tell someone that you will call back, be sure to follow up. If they are difficult to reach, keep trying. It is your responsibility to connect.

9. **Join Professional Organizations**— Visit or join a professional organization in the industry you wish to pursue. Many members are eager to help job seekers and often know employers with open positions.

10. **Get a Mentor**— Find people who have experience in the areas you are pursuing and build a relationship with them. Get their advice and use them as a sounding board for discussing your thoughts and ideas. Ask for an opportunity to shadow them for a day in order to get a better picture of what they do. This may also expose you to new contacts. Be prepared (see point 1).

Introduction
CREATIVE Job Search

There are many reasons why this information is important to you. We live in a constantly changing economy. Corporate reorganizations, new technologies and global competition affect all our lives. Workers today will hold many jobs and will change careers several times. Workers who keep up with change will see greater potential for personal growth and economic security.

One area of change is the way people look for work. It is not enough to be ready and willing to work. A successful job search today requires a very calculated effort. Job seekers not only need marketable job skills, they need the skills to market themselves. You may be motivated toward employment, and you may be good at what you do, but if you cannot convince a potential employer that you are the most qualified, you will not be the one who wins the job. Today's successful job seekers use a variety of skills and strategies that can be learned. The information in this book and in our *Creative Job Search* seminars will assist you in mastering your job search effort. Learning this information will reap proven benefits which include the following:

1. **Shorter time to obtain a new job**
2. **Increase in the number of interviews and job offers**
3. **Higher starting wage**
4. **Reduced fear of unemployment**
5. **Increase in potential for job satisfaction**

Creative Job Search includes materials and seminars offered through the Minnesota WorkForce Center System and Internet resources.
www.MnWorkForceCenter.org

Creative Job Search has been recognized as a premiere resource by job seekers and employment professionals from all over the world. Here are a few of their comments:

"There is so much misinformation about skills on the web. These authors really understand what skills are (refreshing on the Internet)."
   Richard Nelson Bolles, author of *What Color is Your Parachute?*

"Yours has to be one of the best sites on the Internet . . ."
   Job Seeker

"You have, by far, the best information available in America."
   Private Employment Counselor

The Minnesota Department of Economic Security is dedicated to helping you achieve economic security through employment. Minnesota WorkForce Centers throughout Minnesota offer a wide range of employment services. *Creative Job Search* is a progressive curriculum that teaches the skills needed to conduct a successful job search. It is up to you to master these skills. We encourage you to take full advantage of these valuable resources. We wish you success in all your employment endeavors.

—*Creative Job Search Staff*

Transition

It is very hard to move forward if you are always looking backward!

Transition

There is one thing in our lives that remains constant ... *change!* Some changes are good and some bring sadness. Sometimes we are filled with excitement, sometimes dread. No matter what the change, there is a process we go through to successfully handle change.

Change is an event that is situational and continual: the new boss, the new relationship, the new house, the new job. In his book, *Managing Transitions— Making the Most of Change*, William Bridges defines transition as, "The process people go through coming to terms with the new situation." He explains, "change is external," or comes from outside of ourselves. It can be forced or something we choose to do. "Transition is internal." It is our emotional reaction and attitude we use in deciding to accept, adapt, or resist change. Transition usually starts with an ending or the realization that things are not going to stay the same. In order for us to move forward and have some control over the outcome, we need to let go of the past and start exploring all our options and opportunities.

CHANGE

Prior to a change, we were comfortable because our situation was familiar. We resist change due to fear of the unknown. Almost everyone is afraid to make a change. As we move toward new roles and routines, we may experience feelings of fear, anger, sadness, resistance, as well as relief, hope, or excitement. It may feel confusing and chaotic, but it can also be a time of creativity and challenge. What we do with these feelings makes the difference. When we are able to find something positive or see possibilities, we will have energy and motivation to take the next step.

Thoughts + Feelings = Reaction

We choose how to respond to our **thoughts** and **feelings**. This determines our **behavioral** or **emotional reaction** to **change**, whether positive or negative. Think of a recent change you have experienced. What were your thoughts and feelings? How did they influence your reaction? What did you do to get through it?

Attitude

Attitude is everything. It is important to take responsibility for our attitude, because it can give us strength and control during change. Author and multimillionaire W. Clement Stone says, "What the mind can conceive and believe, it can achieve with a positive mental attitude." This is contrary to the current expression, "To have an attitude," which has an opposite, or negative effect. Attitudes are like a magnet. Negative attitudes attract negative results. Positive attitudes attract positive results. Life is not what happens to you, but how you respond to it. You are in charge of your attitude.

Our attitude, whether positive or negative, **shows** in the job search process. Many employers say attitude is more important than experience or education. They often use attitude as the tie breaker between two equally qualified candidates.

Transition

We cannot change the past or how others act, but we can change our attitude. William James, the father of modern psychology, said, "The most important discovery of our time is that we can alter our lives by altering our attitudes." If we learn to manage our attitudes, we will not feel paralyzed, and the benefits will follow.

Creating Your Future

Whether you are unemployed, underemployed, employed but looking for a new job, entering the workforce for the first time, or entering the workforce after a long absence, you are facing change. Change causes transition, and transition starts with an ending. For example, a relationship ends, a job ends, you move, you graduate, or you lose your financial support. Change affects our emotions. You may feel relief, anticipation, renewal, or, you may feel angry, sad, fearful, depressed, or confused. These feelings are natural. Sometimes when endings happen, we grieve. You will survive, but it takes time. Do not deny these feelings, but also do not be driven by them. As you move through transition and accept the facts and find new options, you will feel energetic, productive, and hopeful again.

Positive Attitude Potential

- You will have a better lifestyle for the future
- You are more employable with a positive attitude
- You can be a positive role-model for your children and others
- Your self-esteem will increase along with productivity
- You will have more energy to pursue your goals and dreams

Imagine the Possibilities

- Find meaningful work that fits your skills
- Return to school to learn new skills
- Start your own business
- Follow a dream you have always had
- Re-evaluate your goals and spend time with family
- Meet new people and learn new things

The possibilities are endless.
Look for them.
Make change work for you.

Change Issues

We are all unique and have different concerns about employment.

Roberta is laid off from a major corporation that she worked at for 21 years. She is concerned about finding another job with similar pay and benefits at her age.

Marla has been out of the workforce for 10 years. She is concerned about finding affordable child care, maintaining health benefits, and getting transportation to work.

Terry just graduated from an auto mechanics course at a vocational technical college. He wonders how he will fit in with the experienced mechanics.

Mark is a recently separated veteran with an amputated left arm. He is concerned about marketing his skills and getting a job with his military experience as a radio operator.

What are your issues or concerns about finding work?

Transition

Change of Structure and Routine

When finding yourself in a change situation with your career or job, you may be experiencing transition in several different areas. Perhaps one of the most important things lost or changed when unemployment occurs is **structure**. That is why it is crucial to create and maintain a job search structure for yourself. It will help you stay motivated, on task, and see the steps you need to take to make progress.

Maintain Structure

- Set an alarm clock to get up at your regular time
- Dress as you would for work
- Set aside a place in your home where you do all your job search activity
- Get out of the house and go to the Minnesota WorkForce Center or library, or meet with a job search partner or with a network contact

The following scenarios show how jobs affect our structure and routine and the impact they have on our lives.

Larry called his co-worker, Linda, to talk about the class they are teaching next week. After that, he made dinner, ate, walked the dog, and fell asleep watching television. He awoke remembering he needed to go to work early to catch up on some paper work. He made his lunch, showered, set his alarm for an hour earlier than normal, and climbed into bed. When the alarm rang, he got out of bed and tried to decide what he should wear. He asked himself, "What do I need to do today? Am I seeing customers? Am I teaching class? Do I have meetings to attend? What is the weather going to be like?"

Carla has just accepted her first job, having completed computer training at a vocational school. She is very excited and happy about this opportunity. However, she realizes this means she will need to make some changes to be successful in this job. While she was in school, her 4-year-old daughter was enrolled in the daycare program at school. They took the bus to school three days a week. While Carla was a student, she was able to wear jeans and did not have to arrive until 8:30 a.m.

What will Carla need to do before she starts her new job? Who does she need to contact? What information and arrangements does she need to make before she starts her new job? How did a job change the structure and routine in Larry's and Carla's lives? How would it change your present life structure?

Just think of all the things done or said in these scenarios that are structured by Larry's or Carla's jobs. Job responsibilities dictate when we get up, how we get there, and what clothes we wear. The job may determine where, when, and with whom we eat lunch, and the amount of time we spend away from our children. It also sets the time when we run errands, do laundry, eat supper, and go to bed! When our job situation changes, our routine and lifestyle sometimes change or are even lost. Therefore, it is a good idea to plan ahead, anticipate change, and prepare for the transitions we will go through. This will help us to take positive action, get organized, and accept change in our daily routine, roles, and lives when employed.

Transition

Family Life

While you are unemployed, your family life may be disrupted. Even though you have more time to spend with your family, you feel the constant burden to find a job. Your family is not used to you being at home, and vice versa. They may experience feelings of fear, anger, and confusion about your job situation. Also, sometimes in an attempt to keep things the same, or protect family members' feelings, you avoid talking about your feelings, asking for their ideas, or taking steps to accommodate this situation.

In actuality, it may be an opportunity for a spouse or another member of the household to get a job and develop a career. Children can learn how to earn their own spending money with paper routes, etc., and adult children can take out college loans or pay rent.

When people go to work for the first time, their families and children may need to get used to new routines, tight schedules, getting up earlier, or attending day care. They will need to adjust to the fact that you are not always at home. This can cause chaos for a while, but with time, they will adjust. Their self-esteem may be increased through independence and responsibility.

Social Life

Your job situation may affect your social life. If you have worked at a particular place for a long time, you may have been through many stressful, difficult situations with co-workers. Fellow employees are often close friends. After a job loss, that daily contact may be broken. And, if they are still working, they may be feeling guilty about being employed while you struggle to find a new job. It is not a comfortable situation for either of you. So if you do contact them by phone or meet with them for lunch, you may sense some tension or a feeling that the relationship has changed. The reality is, **it has.**

If you are new to or haven't been in the labor market for a while, your social life also changes. Leaving the comfort and security of home, school, friends, and neighbors is difficult and frightening at first. However, once you are on the job, you will meet new friends and may discover strengths in yourself that may not have been recognized before, like persistence, promptness, resourcefulness, flexibility, dedication, a good phone manner, or a positive attitude.

Income

A job change may affect your ability to support yourself or your family. Your income determines your ability to pay bills, buy groceries, and pursue your hobbies or enjoy leisure time. Not having enough money to pay bills adds **stress.** If you don't deal with this stress, the pressure builds and builds until something just has to give! Developing and keeping a budget will ease your transition through this time and also into the future.

Identity

What we do for a living often defines who we are. When meeting a person for the first time, the question usually asked is, "What do you do?" It is as if by knowing what job a person has, we then know who the person is! What a conversation stopper when you answer, "I'm between jobs right now," or "I'm unemployed," or "I have been a student or a homemaker. Now I am looking for work, but I don't know where or how to find a job because I have no job search or work experience." However, once you have a job, these feelings will change. You will feel you belong.

The Change Cycle

New opportunities, challenges, and rewards come with change. However, with change also comes loss. As with any loss, you may experience varying degrees of sadness, anger, or relief. Trying to move on without recognizing and dealing with the feelings and emotions that arise will make your job search very difficult.

Elisabeth Kubler-Ross, a renowned author and psychiatrist, researched what happens when people suffer loss. She identified five stages of grief that can be similar whenever we feel we have lost something or someone who is important to us. The stages also apply to what you might experience when you lose a job. The person new to the labor market, a recent graduate, a recently separated veteran, or a person with a disability who was unable to work can experience loss of their routine or lifestyle when they begin a job.

Transition

The Change Cycle

Change can be difficult for many

Self-blame
Anger
Denial
Job Transition
Positive Attitude
Depression
New Hope
New Beginning
New Job

Attitude is often the key to transition

Although this is called a cycle, not everyone experiences the emotional ride. However, it is very significant for some, with many ups and downs. You may experience all these emotions or any number of them. Each person's process is unique. The way you handle this process depends on your attitude. Just remember, you must handle this transition before you can move on with your job search.

Transition

The Change Process

Denial
- "I know they will call me back. They will find out how much I contributed and realize that they can't continue without me."
- "My financial support will continue or will be extended."

Anger
- "It's all the company's, the manager's, or the government's fault. I have the right to be really angry about what they did to me. In fact, I was treated so badly, I am going to stay angry for a long, long time! I'll show them that they can't treat me like that! I am not even going to look for work and see how they like that. I am just going to collect benefits. They owe me."

Self-Blame/Depression
- "If only I . . . It's all my fault that I'm in this predicament. I'll never get another job. I don't have enough education. I am not good enough. I am too slow. I don't have any skills, experience, or the right clothes to get a job."
- "I am so worthless. I can't do anything right. I don't even want to get out of bed today. I don't know what is wrong with me. No wonder I can't find a job! Who would want to hire me? I have never done anything before. There are many other people out there who have the experience and education."
- "I should have seen it coming."

Struggle
- "I guess it is time to face the reality that I may need to lower my wage and job expectations. I haven't had much luck finding jobs that will pay me what I was making before, and the jobs in my field seem to have disappeared. When I do get an interview, something always goes wrong."
- "I try to be positive, but it is so hard. Sometimes I just don't know what I am going to do. Maybe if I send out enough resumes, I will get a job."

New Hope
- "What can I learn from this? I accept the facts as they truly are, and I'm ready to move on."
- "My old job is not there. I have skills, abilities, and talents. I'll find something, maybe even better, or I'll try something new."

One thing to remember is each person goes through change differently. The time spent in each stage will vary, as will the sequence of the stages. **No matter how the process plays itself out in your life, it is the right process for you.** Also remember, "this too shall pass" *if* you allow yourself the time to deal with each stage.

Transition

Things That Have Changed

Let's examine the way you are feeling about your employment situation. Now is the time to be truly honest about those feelings.

Many of us were taught that if we worked hard, gave 110 percent to the employer, went the extra mile, and did our very best, the company would take care of us and we would enjoy a comfortable retirement. Suddenly, that was no longer the way companies did things. More and more employers let long-term employees go. Along with the layoff comes the cancellation of life, health, and dental insurance. The pensions some of us were counting on to make retirement dreams come true end up being spent to pay bills for health insurance, mortgage, and car payments. This is not at all what we expected. And even if this was not your plan, whatever happened to being treated fairly?

If you are new to the labor market or haven't worked for a while, you might wonder where the decent paying jobs are. You are ready, available, and looking for work, but there are no jobs.

Exercises

The exercises in this chapter ask you to take an honest look at where you are in the process. They cover some very personal feelings. Therefore, complete them in a place where you feel safe. The exercises do not need to be finished in any given order and they can be "for your eyes only."

Say or write down what is on your mind about your last job. This does not have to be sensible or logical . . . no one else needs to see this. How do you feel about your job situation? Write what you are feeling. Don't censor yourself; just let it out. (If you are having trouble identifying your feelings, the words listed on page 8 might be helpful.)

What changes have occurred in your life over the past 12 months and how do you feel about these changes? The changes may have occurred in your employment situation or in other areas of your life. No matter what the changes may have been, it is valid to look at how you feel about them.

> "To exist is to change, to change is to mature, to mature is to go on creating oneself endlessly."
>
> Henri Bergson, French philosopher

Transition

Feeling Words

Sad
Depressed
Despairing
Disheartened
Dismal
Dismayed
Distressed
Empty
Hopeless
Lonely
Miserable
Mournful
Powerless
Sorrowful
Unhappy

Happy
Calm
Challenged
Cheerful
Confident
Content
Delighted
Ecstatic
Enthusiastic
Excited
Glad
Gleeful
Joyful
Joyous
Optimistic
Peaceful
Proud
Relaxed
Relieved
Satisfied

Scared
Afraid
Alarmed
Anxious
Apprehensive
Fearful
Frightened
Horrified
Insecure
Intimidated
Panicky
Shaken
Terrified
Worried

Confused
Ambivalent
Baffled
Bewildered
Indecisive
Overwhelmed
Perplexed
Puzzled
Troubled
Uncertain
Unfocused
Unsettled
Unsure

Guilty
Apologetic
Regretful
Remorseful

Angry
Aggravated
Agitated
Annoyed
Belligerent
Betrayed
Bitter
Defiant
Disgusted
Exasperated
Frustrated
Furious
Hateful
Hostile
Incensed
Indignant
Infuriated
Irate
Irritated
Mad
Obstinate
Outraged
Peeved
Perturbed
Rageful
Rebellious
Resentful
Seething
Spiteful
Surly
Upset
Vengeful
Vindictive

Ashamed
Embarrassed
Idiotic
Inadequate
Shameful
Worthless

Hurt
Disappointed
Distrustful
Insulted
Victimized
Wounded

Others
Apathetic
Bored
Curious
Defensive
Discontented
Discouraged
Envious
Exhausted
Hesitant
Hopeful
Indifferent
Jealous
Mischievous
Powerful
Restless
Strong
Tense
Tired
Uneasy
Vulnerable

Transition

Things That Have Changed

	What has changed?	I feel …	What was lost?	I feel …	What are the opportunities?	I feel …
1.						
2.						
3.						
4.						
5.						
6.						
7.						
8.						
9.						

Transition

TIPS FOR MANAGING FEELINGS

Talking to Others

Now that you have identified your feelings, how do you deal with them? Talking them out with others often helps. You could talk with a friend, family member, employment or school counselor, minister, social worker, or psychologist (someone you know and trust). Let them know you do not want or necessarily need advice. All feelings are valid and acceptable. You just need to have someone listen to you. Ask for constructive feedback if you want it.

Support Groups

If you have a support group or job club in your area, do not hesitate to attend. It can provide you with much needed nonjudgmental support from others going through the same things. You may also find valuable tips, job leads, and an opportunity to network and get new ideas. Inquire at your Minnesota WorkForce Center or local employment service for dates, times, and locations of support groups.

Writing a Letter

If you are uncomfortable expressing your feelings, try writing them down. Write a letter to your former boss, telling her/him exactly how you are feeling. Write down how you are feeling about starting to look for work and the changes it has brought. Don't worry about the content or structure of the letter, because you are not going to send it. Writing it down may release some anger you might be experiencing. This will help restore the feeling that you are in control of your life. After you have written the letter, read it aloud, and then dispose of it. You could rip it up into small pieces and then burn it. You could wad it up into a ball, bat it around outside, and then throw it in the trash. Just do something to get rid of it. A recent study found that people who write about their anger get another job faster than those who don't.

Deep Breathing

When you have completed writing your letter(s), sit down with both feet on the floor, close your eyes, take a long, deep breath, picture a peaceful, pleasant place, then exhale completely. Repeat until you feel relaxed and calm.

Transition

Physical Exercise

Anger is a natural emotion, but it can be destructive. Therefore, we need to recognize it and take steps to control it. One way to handle anger or negative feelings is by doing something physical. You could go outside and exercise, play basketball, take a vigorous walk, go bowling, play baseball or tennis, work-out, or clean the house, garage, or car. You can decide to walk away from your aggravating situation by doing something else like positive self-talk, counting to 100, diverting your attention, or talking to someone.

As you use these positive ways of dealing with your feelings, your anxiety will lessen, and your health and mood will improve. You will not be as likely to take things out on your family, friends, or pets. However, if you feel you cannot contain your anger and may hurt yourself or others, put your children in a safe place, then call your local crisis center.

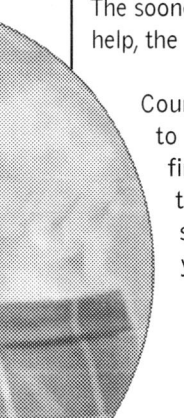

Face Your Fears

It is normal for everyone to be afraid of something, but fear can be our biggest enemy. If we allow it to rule our lives, it can keep us from realizing our goals, dreams, and true potential. Fear can make false events appear real. Sometimes we create excuses for ourselves so we do not have to face our fears and take a risk. For example, "No one will hire me because I am . . . too old, lack experience, have been on welfare, etc." These things do not have to stop you.

Counseling

It is necessary to work through emotions. You can get stuck in your emotions and create negative patterns that will hinder your job search and career. If the previous suggestions do not help you handle your anger, depression, fears, or anxiety so you are able to do an active job search, it is a good idea to talk with a professional counselor, psychologist or psychiatrist. Everyone's stress level and pressures are different. Do not be reluctant to get the help you need. The sooner you take action to get help, the sooner you will feel better.

Counseling can be very helpful to broaden your perspective, find new ways of looking at the situation, and get the support and encouragement you need.

Dealing with Fear

- Recognize everyone is afraid of something.

- Identify your fears. Figure out exactly what you are afraid of (rejection, success, failure, or what others might say). Naming your fear can reduce its power.

- Talk with someone you trust. Are you being realistic in your own self-evaluation?

- Recall your strengths and successes. How have you handled other fearful situations?

- Evaluate how likely your fears will become reality. If the worst happens, how terrible will it be?

- Write an action plan to ensure it will not happen. Fear is absence of a plan. Action is the best remedy.

- Take a low-risk action. If you fear interviewing, practice interviewing with a friend or counselor.

- Use affirmations and self-talk. Visualize a positive, successful outcome.

- Face your fears. Take the risk. You can do it! You are ready. Go for it! Remember, Babe Ruth struck out many more times than he made home runs. Abraham Lincoln had many setbacks before he was elected president.

After you have confronted your fears, you will be surprised how your confidence will be strengthened.

CREATIVE Job Search

Transition

Resources

Check with your Minnesota WorkForce Center, local employment service, or local county information referral center to obtain a listing of local resources that can help you during this time. The list may include free job search support groups and area agencies that can provide help. For example, in Minnesota, the United Way operates **First Call for Help**, a resource available 24-hours a day.

Y ou can't sell yourself to a new employer if you are still angry with the last one!

Stress Management Techniques

People are often unsuccessful in their job search because they have not dealt with their feelings surrounding a job change. If not dealt with, feelings have a way of creating stress, and can sometimes cause illness. Therefore, it is extremely important to use healthy ways of handling stress. Here are some suggestions.

Put a checkmark by the techniques you can do during your job search.

- ☐ Get organized— create a structure for your job search.
- ☐ Exercise daily— walk, run, jog, swim, bike, dance, etc.
- ☐ Eat healthy— eat three balanced meals a day.
- ☐ Reduce— junk food, sugar, caffeine, and watching television.
- ☐ Avoid— alcohol, drugs, and smoking.
- ☐ Stay positive— use positive self-talk, affirmations, list your strengths, be with supportive people.
- ☐ Get plenty of sleep.
- ☐ Write— in a journal or diary your thoughts and feelings, what you learn, and your progress.
- ☐ Take a warm bath— it calms you and gives you time alone.
- ☐ Attend job support groups or clubs— share ideas, tips, stresses, accept and give praise.
- ☐ Be flexible— stay open to new ideas, think creatively, take risks.
- ☐ Take one thing at a time. Plan and prioritize.
- ☐ Moderation— make one change at a time. Many changes add stress.
- ☐ Relax daily— take time to do something you enjoy.
- ☐ Reward yourself— when you accomplish certain job search activities and goals.
- ☐ Learn something new.
- ☐ Accept— what you cannot change, change what you can, forgive self and others.
- ☐ Be thankful— find things to be thankful for.
- ☐ Say NO— when you need to take care of yourself, set limits with friends and family.
- ☐ Express feelings— laugh or cry, admit your true feelings to yourself and someone you trust.
- ☐ Volunteer— doing something for others increases your self esteem, your network, and your skills.
- ☐ Find humor— watch comedies and comedians, children at play, and find time for play.
- ☐ Manage time— keep schedules, set goals and time tables, use a calendar.
- ☐ Meditate— on your own spiritual truths or on peaceful thoughts.
- ☐ Visualize— achieving your goals, your future position, your role, and situations to come.

Transition

Identity Worksheet

Who are you? It is easy to respond by naming the roles we play. But do those roles truly define us? If someone says "mommy," what do you really know about the person? The same is true if the person were a secretary, doctor, construction worker, or teacher. Since our roles in life often change, we can maintain a healthy self-image by learning to recognize ourselves apart from those roles.

In the following exercise, think about how you would describe yourself without using the roles you fill. For example, a person might say they were sociable, stubborn, and thoughtful. Maybe they would use words such as mystical, confident, and playful. Use words that you feel truly describe you.

I am _____

I am _____

I am _____

I am _____

I am _____

I am _____

I am _____

I am _____

I am _____

I am _____

I am _____

I am _____

I am _____

I am _____

I am _____

I am _____

Transition

MAKING ENDS MEET

Let's be honest. When we find ourselves unemployed or underemployed, the most pressing thought is how we are going to pay the bills! It is hard to survive in today's world with little or no money. There are some practical things you can do to keep your head above water.

First, develop a realistic budget. By doing this you will find out just how much and to whom you owe money. Listed below are some steps to setting up a budget.

1) Using the worksheets on pages 16 and 17, gather all your bills. Go through each of them and record the name of the creditor, the total amount you owe, and the amount of any monthly payments.

2) List any bills that are not due monthly, such as car insurance or water bills. Looking through your checkbook will help you to remember these bills.

3) Consider all the items you purchase with checks (food, rent, entertainment, gas, medication, etc.). Review your checkbook for common expenses. Write all these down.

4) When you have listed all your bills, compare the amount you owe each month with the amount of income you will have. Don't be discouraged if you have more in the outgoing column than in the incoming. We will provide you with some suggestions about how to pay these bills.

5) Take a good, hard look at your expenses. Are there obvious places where you can cut corners? How about the number of times you have eaten out in the past month? How many trips to the store resulted in your purchasing only items you absolutely needed? Can you reduce entertainment expenses? It is important to allow yourself some entertainment each week, but it doesn't always have to cost money. Consider items you can cut and items that must remain in your budget.

6) Now that you have cut some "fat" out of your expenses, consider what you can truly spend on the bills you have. For example, if you have a credit card bill with a minimum monthly payment of $100, can you pay $50 or $75 each month? Don't worry about the credit card company yet, just put down what you think you can afford to pay. After you have done that, read the outgoing expenses column and compare it to your income. Getting closer?

7) Once you have the income and expense columns equal, contact your creditors and explain what is happening. Let them know your intentions to put forth a good-faith effort by continuing payments on these accounts. Making these contacts with creditors can help to maintain a better credit rating.

8) If you want more advice on budgeting during this time, contact the nearest University of Minnesota Extension Office, Minnesota WorkForce Center, or local employment service. They can give you valuable information and helpful suggestions.

9) If you need credit advice, contact the Consumer Credit Counseling Service, a nonprofit service in some communities.

10) If you owe child support, check to see if your county has a "Parent's Fair Share Program" for financial assistance.

11) Save your receipts, because some job search expenses can be deducted from your income tax.

12) If you are receiving **Unemployment Insurance (UI)**, you are required to report on your tax forms the amount of UI you receive during the filing year. Depending on the amount of other income you earned during the filing year, you may be required to pay income tax on the UI. It is a good idea to contact the Internal Revenue Office or other tax professionals when estimating the amount you may need to put aside for payment of this tax. You can choose to have taxes withheld from your UI benefits.

Transition

Tips For Saving Money

- Use public transportation, ride-share, or car-pool.

- Find low-cost auto repairs. Some vocational schools do auto repairs at reduced prices.

- Have a garage sale.

- Rent out an extra room.

- Sell the adult toys (boat, jet ski, snowmobile, cabin).

- Sell collections or the extra car.

- Check your investments and insurance policies. You may be over-insured or can increase your deductible. Your credit cards may have a clause that will pay your minimum monthly balance while you are unemployed.

- Make gifts instead of buying them.

- Work odd jobs, take part-time or temporary work, or become an independent contractor.

- Teach your skills at community education centers or to other local groups.

- Sell your arts and crafts.

- For recent graduates, get a deferment on school loans until you find a job.

- Shop at discount stores and thrift shops.

- Go to the dollar movies, rent movies, or borrow them from the public library.

- Use discount coupons, or share services like baby-sitting, repairs, typing, or rides.

- Attend concerts, museums, and art galleries on reduced price days.

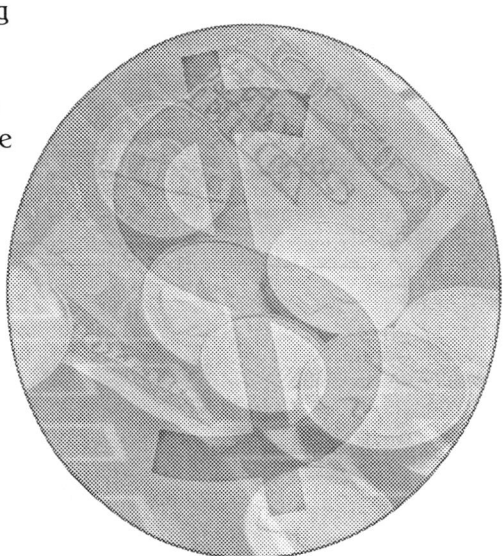

Transition Budget Worksheet

INCOME	PRESENT INCOME	ANTICIPATED INCOME
Wages/Unemployment Insurance	$	$
Interest		
Savings		
Child Support		
Loans		
Other		
Monthly Total	$	$

EXPENSES	PRESENT EXPENSES	ANTICIPATED EXPENSES
HOUSEHOLD		
Rent/Mortgage		
Furnishings/Equipment		
Maintenance/Repair		
Taxes		
UTILITIES		
Electricity		
Heat		
Water/Sewer		
Telephone		
FOOD & GROCERIES		
Food at Home		
School/Work Lunch		
TRANSPORTATION		
Car Payment		
Gas		
Maintenance/Repair		
Bus/Taxi		
MEDICAL		
Doctor/Dentist		
Prescriptions		
MONTHLY TOTAL	$	$

CREATIVE Job Search

Transition Budget Worksheet

EXPENSES	PRESENT EXPENSES	ANTICIPATED EXPENSES
CHILD CARE		
CLOTHING		
Laundry/Dry Cleaning		
PERSONAL CARE		
Hair Care		
INSURANCE		
Automobile		
Home/Renter's		
Life		
Medical		
RECREATION & ENTERTAINMENT		
Cable TV		
Movies/Rental Movies		
Magazines/Newspapers		
Cigarettes/Alcohol		
Gambling/Lottery		
Eating Out		
GIFTS		
CONTRIBUTIONS		
INSTALLMENTS		
Department Store Credit Cards		
Bank Charge Cards		
Loans		
CHILD SUPPORT		
Children's School Expenses		
JOB SEARCH		
Postage		
Copies		
Resume Paper/Supplies		
MISCELLANEOUS		
MONTHLY TOTAL	$	$

CREATIVE Job Search

Transition

Affirmations

Affirmations can help you obtain your goals and dreams. Repeating positive statements about yourself will help you stay focused, motivated, and create ways to achieve your goals. If you repeat them out loud several times a day, you will believe them and avoid falling into negative self-talk and actions. Since your thoughts and beliefs direct your actions, you will feel good about yourself, look confident, and have a sense of control over your future. Choose one affirmation each day to use in all your activities. See if you become more positive about yourself and your life. Try writing your own unique affirmations.

- I am in charge of my own life and fully able to change
- I am talented and capable
- I am capable of meeting any challenge
- I repeat affirmations daily to stay motivated and achieve my goals
- I am happy, healthy, and calm
- I am full of enthusiasm and vitality
- I am proud of myself because . . .
- I am learning not to blame
- I set goals in every area of my life and review them daily
- I focus on my strengths, accomplishments, and goals
- I succeed by making the most of my time
- I am taking control of my thoughts and my life
- I choose the way I respond to outside events
- I take action that will improve my self-image
- I have a clear mental picture of my goals and ideals
- I am relaxed, confident, and creative
- I am successful in my job search because I believe in myself and my goals
- Every day, in every way, I am getting closer to my goals

"What to Keep" Worksheet

Now that you have looked at your budget, consider what you need to keep and what has to go. Most of us think about eliminating entertainment and hobbies when money gets tight. This may not be a good idea. You may need to keep activities that provide a release from tension and stress. For example, now may not be the time to give up your health club membership. Working out is one way to reduce stress and maintain a positive outlook. Looking your very best as you are seeking employment may require keeping your appointment with the hair stylist/barber. Staying in touch with co-workers and friends is an excellent way to network during this time. Perhaps you will want to continue having lunch with them occasionally.

List the activities in your life that provide relief from stress, that help maintain a good self-image, that enable you to continue communicating with people, etc. Then decide if the activity is one you can keep in your schedule— or not.

Activity	Keep or Not
1. _____	_____
2. _____	_____
3. _____	_____
4. _____	_____
5. _____	_____
6. _____	_____
7. _____	_____
8. _____	_____
9. _____	_____
10. _____	_____

Transition

NOTES

Transition

NOTES

CREATIVE Job Search 20

Job Search Preparation

Be prepared...
a must for every
job seeker.

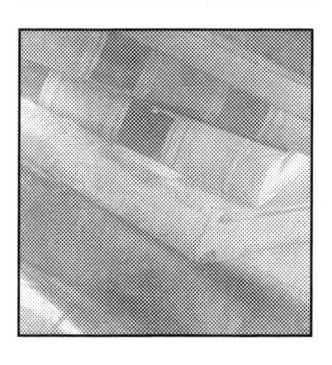

Job Search Preparation

ORGANIZATION

A successful job search requires organization and effort. You cannot simply walk out the door and wander around asking about jobs. Nor can you look for work only when you feel like it or when it is convenient.

Planning and organizing are critical to job search success. For those who are accustomed to self-directed activities, this will not be difficult. But for those who are used to having someone else organize their activities, this will require mastering new skills. You may not consider yourself an organized person, but you can learn this skill. Organizing your job search will save you time and effort. Good self-management and organization skills are valuable resources no matter what your experience might be.

You will need to develop a new routine to be successful in your job search. You may have to create a new set of priorities and schedules. Be aware that there will be many things that will distract you. Just about anything will sound better than looking for work. Don't be fooled; your number one priority is finding that new job. **Don't let anything get in your way.**

Time and Job Hunting

Before we look at the finer points of organizing a job search, we need to make something clear: looking for work is hard work! It takes time and energy to be successful. Most people work a 40-hour week. If you are unemployed, those hours are available for your job search. If you are employed but seeking new opportunities, you need to make time for your job search. Be consistent in the amount of time you spend each week looking for a job. Don't spend 40 hours one week and then nothing for the next two weeks! The hardest part is getting started. Once you get the momentum into your search, you will want to keep moving forward.

Don't think of yourself as unemployed. You have a job— a full-time job. If you are employed, think of your job search as a part-time job. You are engaged in a very calculated sales and marketing campaign designed to sell your skills and experience to a prospective employer. You are now self-employed; you are the boss. It's up to you to make sure the job gets done. Set your schedule and stick to it. The only reasons you would not conduct your job search would be the same reasons you would use for not going to work.

Job Search Preparation

Advance Scheduling

Successful job seekers have mastered the art of managing their schedules. Job search scheduling and goal setting should be done daily and weekly. **Establish measurable goals.** For example, block out the hours you have committed to the search and identify what you plan to accomplish. If you set 9-11 a.m., Monday, for library research, your goal could be to identify 10 new employers you can pursue. Tuesday's goal could be contacting the 10 new employers you identified Monday. Tuesday, 1-3 p.m., may be scheduled for making direct telephone contacts. Be realistic, but challenge yourself.

Make Yourself Accountable

Create an area in your home where all of your job search is centered. This will help you feel like looking for a job when you are in that area. If you keep all your job search equipment, supplies, and information there, you will stay organized and ready to look for work.

Check your progress at the end of each day and week. See if you accomplished your goals. When you do, commend yourself and decide if you can set tougher goals next time. If you didn't accomplish the goals, explore why and decide what you need to do to succeed in the future. Maybe your goals were not realistic; you tried to do too much. Learn from this and plan more realistic goals for the future. It may be a good strategy to involve someone else in your search. Talk with a trusted friend; give them permission to hold you accountable to your plans. Attending a job club would also enable you to discuss your job search with others.

Keep Accurate Records

If you are conducting a serious job campaign, you may make hundreds of contacts and generate new opportunities daily. Do not simply rely on your memory. You need to have and maintain a filing system, just as you would make a grocery or "To Do" list. There are a variety of systems you can use including alphabetized three-ring binders, small pocket calendars, and notebooks. Check your local office supply or discount store for examples. Just keep it easy to use and maintain.

People don't plan to fail, they fail to plan.

Job Search Preparation

Job Seeking Activity Goals

Filling out this sheet will help you plan and achieve your job goals.

Period: _____ to _____

Activity	Goal (# or date)	Actual (# or date)
Contact Minnesota WorkForce Center (WFC)	_____	_____
Familiarize yourself with the WFC Resource Area	_____	_____
Review electronic job search tools	_____	_____
Attend job search training sessions or related training	_____	_____
Research employers/go to library	_____	_____
Attend support groups/job clubs	_____	_____
Read local newspapers	_____	_____
Read trade journals	_____	_____
Read other publications	_____	_____
Contact network	_____	_____
Make cold calls (phone/in person)	_____	_____
Complete/update resume	_____	_____
Send cover letters/resumes sent	_____	_____
Attend job fairs	_____	_____
Participate in informational interviewing	_____	_____
Talk to someone every day about your job search	_____	_____
Attend professional organizations	_____	_____
Talk to your references/write reference sheet	_____	_____
Make follow-up phone calls	_____	_____
Follow-up on job leads	_____	_____
Interview with employer	_____	_____
Send thank you/follow-up letters	_____	_____
Others:		
_____	_____	_____
_____	_____	_____
_____	_____	_____

CREATIVE Job Search

Job Search Preparation

Sample Job Search Schedule

Week of **September 7**

Time	Sunday	Monday	Tuesday	Wednesday	Thursday	Friday	Saturday
8:00	Shower and dress. Pick up newspaper. Read the "fun" stuff first.	Shower and dress by 8:30. Set goals for the day/week.	Same as Monday.	Same as Monday.	Same as Monday.	Same as Monday.	Go to the farmers' market.
9:00	Read Sunday paper. Get to the ads by 9:30.	Respond by phone to Sunday ads.	Make networking calls.	Return calls, schedule appointments.	Attend Job Club.	Return calls & schedule appointments.	
10:00	Take a walk, play with the kids, etc.	Get info for writing responses to ads. Go to the Minnesota WorkForce Center.	Make networking calls.	Attend Job Fair.	Attend Job Club.	Make networking calls.	
11:00	Have some fun!	Write cover letters, changes on resume.	Return phone calls, schedule appointments.		Do informational interview.		
12:00	Lunch	Lunch	Lunch	Lunch	Lunch	Lunch	Lunch
1:00		Appointment	Appointment	Check out Minnesota WorkForce Center computer.	Appointment	Research the company for the interview next week.	
2:00		Appointment	Appointment	Call on leads obtained at Minnesota WorkForce Center.	Appointment	Research the company for the interview next week.	
3:00		Appointment	Appointment	Appointment		Research the company for the interview next week.	
4:00		Walk	Walk	Walk	Walk	Walk	
5:00		Evaluate today. Review tomorrow. Send thank you notes.	Same as Monday.	Same as Monday.	Same as Monday.	Same as Monday, and review the week.	

CREATIVE Job Search 24

Job Search Preparation

Job Search Schedule

Week of _____

TIME	SUNDAY	MONDAY	TUESDAY	WEDNESDAY	THURSDAY	FRIDAY	SATURDAY
8:00							
9:00							
10:00							
11:00							
12:00							
1:00							
2:00							
3:00							
4:00							
5:00							

CREATIVE Job Search

Job Search Preparation

Networking Log

It is important to document and follow-up all job leads. Use this sheet for keeping track of all your networking activity. Always ask if your contacts will suggest another contact. Keep the ball rolling!

Contact Name: _____ Date Called: _____

Company Name: _____

Address: _____

Action Plan: _____

Fax: _____ Appointment Date/Time: _____

E-Mail Address: _____

Follow-up: _____

_____

_____

Summary of Conversation/Contact: _____

_____

_____

_____

_____

Contact Names Received

In making your network contact, did you receive other job leads? If so, list them below.

Name: _____   Name: _____

Position: _____   Position: _____

Company: _____   Company: _____

Phone: _____   Phone: _____

Fax/E-Mail: _____   Fax/E-Mail: _____

Name: _____   Name: _____

Position: _____   Position: _____

Company: _____   Company: _____

Phone: _____   Phone: _____

Fax/E-Mail: _____   Fax/E-Mail: _____

CREATIVE Job Search

Job Search Preparation

Job Lead Worksheet

No matter where you get your job leads, it is important to keep track of them. Follow-up on each lead, which may provide you with other job leads. Do not be afraid to ask for other contacts or leads.

Company: _____

Contact Person: _____

Address: _____

Phone: _____

Fax/E-Mail Address: _____

Position: _____

How did I find out about this job? _____

_____

Response: _____

Sent or faxed resume on: _____

Date called: _____

Follow-up date: _____

Results and other useful information: _____

_____

_____

_____

_____

_____

_____

CREATIVE Job Search

Job Search Preparation

DISCOVER WHERE THE JOBS ARE

Research is another important part of your preparation. When some people hear the word "research," they have visions of a mad scientist surrounded by test tubes, microscopes, and Bunsen burners. Others might think of endless trips to the library where they have to read stacks of books. The type of research needed in the job search is not what you might think.

Why do research at all? When you research an industry, occupation, or employer, you gain the information you need to make a good decision about the direction of your job search. You get to decide whether to apply for a job at a specific employer based on facts, not on feelings. You are in control. The information you gain while conducting this research will also impress the prospective employer during the interview. It says you are serious about your job search. Research can be done on occupations, industries, individual companies, availability of jobs in your area, and on other topics.

Research does not have to be time-consuming. You don't have to check out 25 books from a library. Research can be as simple as looking at newspaper employment ads. Newspaper ads, the Internet, company brochures, and company Internet home pages can be good resources for discovering what experience, training, and knowledge are required by a variety of employers. You can measure your qualifications against those required by the employer. Do you need to get more training in a certain area? Does your resume cover the qualifications most requested by the employer?

Benefits of Research

- Increased job search confidence
- Increased control over the job search
- Increased decision-making ability
- Increased potential for job search success
- Increased employment satisfaction
- Increased potential for economic security

Researching an Employer

Before you apply for a job at a particular employer, you should learn as much about that employer as you can. Researching the employer will give you the information you need when deciding if this is an employer for which you would like to work. Would employment with them meet your career values?

Sources of Published Information

- Library
- Internet
- Telephone Yellow Pages
- Professional/trade associations and unions
- Business and Manufacturer Guide
- Dunn & Bradstreet Directory
- Standard and Poors
- Corporate Report Fact Book
- Corporate Yellow Book
- Business Almanac
- Business Directory
- Employer database such as InfoTrac at local libraries
- News articles about employers
- Business Periodicals Index

Job Search Preparation

John was looking for a welding job, although he had very little work experience. He did not think it was necessary to do research as he had an interview already set up with a small employer. After completing his job search training, he decided it might be to his benefit to research the employer. After researching, he went to his interview. One of the first questions asked of him was: "Tell me what you know about this company." Since he had done the research, he was able to impress the interviewer with the knowledge he had learned. The very next day John was offered the welding job.

Listed below are some of the many **sources** that have information about employers.

- Minnesota WorkForce Center Resource Area staff, or staff at your local employment service.

- People who are working for the employer.

- Current newspapers, trade journals, and business magazines. Older copies of these can also be found in library archives.

- Internet: Employer home pages often include extensive information including their vision, mission statement, product descriptions, hiring policies, and job openings. Articles in Internet publications contain information that relates to industries, occupations, or employers. Internet newsgroups and e-mail are excellent resources for networking.

- Libraries: Most have special sections on occupations, careers, and job search information. Talk to your librarian about newspaper indexes, which list recent articles about employers.

- Colleges and university placement offices.

- Chamber of Commerce or Jaycees.

- Alumni Associations.

- Annual reports, advertisements, employer newsletters and brochures. Often you can obtain these by contacting the employer's public relations office or personnel department.

Here are some sample questions:

- What products/services does the employer provide?

- How many employees does the company have?

- How long have they been in business?

- Where is the employer located? Does it have more than one location? Is it on the bus line?

- What is the employer's mission statement or philosophy?

- What is the company's financial situation? Is it making money?

- Has the employer undergone any downsizing in the last five years?

- Is the employer involved in community services? If so, what?

29 CREATIVE Job Search

Job Search Preparation

Labor Market Survey

The purpose of a labor market survey is to figure out if an occupation or specific line of work is appropriate for you. A labor market survey may be conducted over the telephone, by e-mail, or on Internet newsgroups. You will want to find out about:

- Competition for available job openings
- Background and training requirements
- Prevailing wages
- Future trends of the occupation

Talking with people currently working in the occupation you are interested in is one way of getting up-to-date information about this occupation.

You will need to have a clear idea of the specific occupation or line of work that interests you. You can clarify an occupational definition by consulting the *Occupational Information Network (O*Net)*, Minnesota Career Information System (MCIS), or other reference books available at Minnesota WorkForce Centers or your local employment service, public libraries, technical schools, colleges, and universities.

Conducting a Labor Market Survey

- Identify people with knowledge about the job or occupation you are investigating. *Vocational Biographies*, business directories, the yellow pages, Internet newsgroups, and Internet home pages are useful sources for contact information.

- Contact each person on your list. Direct your inquiries to people knowledgeable about hiring practices. Say you are seeking **advice** and **information**, and that you will be brief. Explain you are seeking career information, not employment. Most people are willing to interact for a short time. It may be necessary, however, to check back. Try to get a name, then ask the person when would be a good time for you to check back.

- Prepare a short list of questions (3-5).
  - What are the background and training requirements for this occupation?
  - How many applicants do you usually have for a job opening in this field?
  - How many have you hired in the last year?
  - What is the typical entry-level wage?
  - What is the typical top wage?
  - What are the future trends for this field?
  - What recommendations could you give for someone who is considering this field?

- Write down the key comments.

- Your survey results will be more reliable if you contact several people. Contact between six to 10 people to obtain a valid sample.

- If a phone conversation is going well, you could ask if the person is willing to meet for a longer, face-to-face interview. Also ask if there is anyone else you could contact.

- Review your notes. Notice which comments were the most optimistic, the most pessimistic, and whether there is agreement from those you contacted. You may want to do other research, including reading, doing in-person interviews, observing the job being done ("job shadowing"), or sampling tasks of the job.

Informational Interviewing

What is it?

It is **not** an interview for a position. It is a meeting of usually 15 to 30 minutes with a person who has hands-on experience in the area you want to know more about. The purpose of an informational interview is to help you define your career options. It is also useful in researching companies where you may want to work.

Informational Interviewing Objectives

- To gain solid information that will help you evaluate how your skills and interests dovetail with a particular career or business.

- To learn what the industry or employer values in its employees.

- To increase your network by leaving a positive impression with someone who could provide encouragement, support, and future access to job leads.

- To find out whether jobs are available in the field or business you want to enter.

- To find out suggestions they have about the career or the employer.

- To market your skills, subtly leave a copy of your resume in case they want to contact you when an opening occurs. Ask if they think your resume would be appropriate for their employer or this occupation.

Be sure they do not get the impression you are asking them for a job! Don't misrepresent yourself either. Be honest.

CREATIVE Job Search 30

Job Search Preparation

Who to contact:

Everyone you know.
Ask, "Do you know anyone who works for General Mills?" "Do you know anyone in a nonprofit organization?" "Do you know anyone who does freelance writing?"
Then once you have a name . . .

> "Mrs. Smith, Brad Johnson suggested I speak with you. My name is Steven Olson and I am interested in the _____ field. I could use some advice from someone who is in this field. Do you have any time this week when I could meet with you? I know you are busy, so I only need about 15 minutes of your time. I would really like to learn more about your company and the _____ field from someone like you."

You may also want to explain a little about your employment background and why this area is appealing to you.

Preparing for the Interview:

Select questions relating to the occupation or business you are considering. Research key areas of potential discussion. Take an active role in the interview. Encourage suggestions. Ask questions that provide the information you want. Show your interest and knowledge.

Keep in mind that you can also ask about other things. Get a sense for whether they enjoy their work. Decide what they actually do, how they spend their day, and what their short- and long-term responsibilities are. Look for the answers behind the answers.

Develop rapport with the interviewer by recognizing similar interests and being agreeable. It is important to gauge just how friendly your contacts really are. If they're sympathetic, you can ask hard questions which may reveal doubts about the field. If they are standoffish or judgmental, be cautious. Don't be afraid to ask technical questions, especially if it shows what you already know about the field. The Informational Interview Worksheet on page 33 lists questions that you may want to ask.

When you go:

This is an opportunity to meet a person in the profession you are hoping to enter. Dress professionally, take paper for writing notes, and take an extra resume in case there is an opportunity to have it critiqued or to leave it with the employer.

Avoid anything that might jeopardize your interviewer's desire to refer you to other people. One important objective is getting additional leads and referrals, which may eventually lead to a job.

When it is over:

- You should have names of people to contact.
- You should follow-up on the advice the employer gives you.
- You should have a good idea if this is where you would want to work or could work.
- Recap what you just learned or need to learn.
- Write down additional notes/thoughts/evaluation for future reference.
- **Don't forget to send a thank you note** to the person for being so generous with their time. Also include your personal calling card:

```
ACCOUNTANT | JUSTIN TIME
             111 Job Avenue
             St. Paul, MN 55555
             (651) 555-5555

             Accountant
             Six years of experience

             Fax: (651) 444-4444
             E-Mail: justin.time@rrr.com
```

- Ask for a business card which will give you the information needed for the thank you note.

Job Search Preparation

Research and Labor Market Information Worksheet

Company Name: _____

Address: _____

Type of Business: _____ Year Business Started: _____

Financial Status: _____

Number of Employees: _____

Product and Services Description: _____

Name of Contact Person: _____

Date Contacted: _____ Date to Follow-up: _____

Other subsidiaries: _____

What are the background and training requirements for this occupation? _____

How many applicants do you usually have for a job opening in this field? _____

How many employees have you hired in the last year? _____

What is the typical entry-level wage for this occupation? _____

What is the typical top wage? _____

What recommendations could you give for someone who is considering or may be entering this field? _____

CREATIVE Job Search

Job Search Preparation

Informational Interview Worksheet

Take this worksheet with you when you are doing your informational interviews with employers. Be positive, friendly, and show your gratitude. You may want to make a copy of this page before you start your informational interviewing.

What is a typical day on this job really like? _____

How did you get into this field? _____

What do you like about your jobs? Any dislikes? _____

What's the best way to find out about jobs in this field? _____

What kind of experience or training is required? _____

What is the career ladder for this position? _____

May I have a copy of a job description? _____

What are employers looking for (skills, education, experience)? _____

How important is the resume and what makes one impressive? _____

What do you look for in employees? _____

How do you stay current in your knowledge? _____

What's the corporate culture like here? _____

Are there related fields I might want to look into if few jobs are available in my primary career goal? _____

What are current job prospects like? _____

What are the most important parts of your job? _____

Is your job typical of others in this field? _____

Which firms do you think are your toughest competitors, and how do they differ from your company? _____

Is there anyone else you can refer me to in this field? _____

How do you normally hire for this occupation? _____

What is the average turnover in this type of job? _____

Is my resume appropriate for this occupation? _____

What would you recommend I do at this point to get into this field? _____

33 CREATIVE Job Search

Job Search Preparation

NOTES

Skills Identification

The Foundation of a Successful Job Search.

Skills Identification

Skills are the foundation of an effective job search. Employers do not just want to know where you have been and what your job titles were. They want to know what you can do. If you were planning to purchase a product that would cost thousands of dollars annually, you would want to know what it can do.

The average person has between 500 and 800 skills! You need to identify at least five to 10 skills that are the **most** attractive to potential employers. Many people have a hard time identifying their skills. Do not think of a skill as something that requires years of formal education and experience to develop. A skill is anything you can do right now!

A Lesson From Sales

Looking for work is selling a product. A successful job search is a sales and marketing campaign. To successfully sell a product, a salesperson must know as much as possible about that product. The same is true for your job search.

Consider a major purchase you made or are planning to make: a car, appliances, a computer, or stereo equipment. If you are a smart consumer, you will shop around. You ask questions. You want to know what sets a product apart from the competition. It is the salesperson's job to convince the buyer that their product is the best. This is why salespeople spend many hours learning their products. This is also why you need to invest time in identifying your skills.

SKILLS AND TASKS

Skills are those activities that you can do right now. They include very specific activities such as sewing, record keeping, cooking, cleaning, computer programming, and welding. We call these skills **job-specific skills**. Skills also include less specific activities such as being on time, dependable, independent, flexible, and ambitious. We call these skills **self-management skills**.

A combination of skills are used together to accomplish a task. We accomplish many tasks each day. A combination of tasks make up an activity. Activities may be part of a job, volunteer work, hobbies, recreation, or daily life. Think of an activity as describing a major area of responsibility that requires a set of tasks. Some tasks are related to employment. A secretary writes a letter. A computer programmer proofreads computer codes. A cook prepares vegetables. Other tasks are accomplished in the course of our daily lives. Balancing a checking account, shopping, driving, and mowing the lawn are all examples of tasks. Tasks are part of our recreation, hobbies, and volunteer work. There is not one right way to apply these concepts. Each situation will be unique. Many times skills and tasks seem interchangeable. That's because they are describing the same thing— the elements of an activity. They simply look at the activity from different levels. It's up to you to apply these principles to your own experiences.

Job Skills

Job skills are those skills specific to a job or occupation. An administrative assistant is skilled in typing, word processing, answering telephones and company correspondence, and filing. An accountant's skills would include calculating accounts receivable and accounts payable, preparing taxes, and using computer accounting programs. A salesperson's skills would include customer service, record keeping, order processing, inventory management, billing, and product displays.

Behind most skills lies a body of knowledge. The person performing computer programming has learned a computer language such as Visual Basic. A cook knows about cooking techniques such as basting or baking. These bodies of knowledge are also skills.

Skills are the performance specifications of your product— you.

Skills Identification

Job skills are important to employers for obvious reasons. They are the specific skills employers look for in a candidate. Job skills do not always come from employment. They may be developed through education, hobbies, community activities, and life experiences. Common activities such as shopping, managing finances, balancing a bank account, hosting a party, and teaching a child all contain potential job skills.

Activity	Task	Potential Skills
Shopping	Shopping List	Planning/organizational skills, Budgeting, Time management, Product evaluation, Determining nutrition, etc.
Yard Work	Lawn Care	Physical endurance/coordination, Equipment maintenance, Safety operations, Chemical applications, etc.

Self-Management Skills

These are skills you use day-to-day to get along with others to survive. They are the skills that make you unique. Sincerity, reliability, tactfulness, patience, flexibility, timeliness, and tolerance are all examples of self-management skills. Motivational attributes and attitudes are also self-management skills. Persistence, drive, and cooperation are examples. Do not underestimate self-management skills, especially those that show motivation and a good work attitude. Employers look for these skills to determine how a candidate will fit into the organization. How a person will fit in is an important consideration for employers. These skills are especially important for people who are seeking their first job or returning to employment after an absence.

Transferable Skills

Many skills can be applied to a variety of activities. They can transfer from one activity to another. Self-management skills are highly transferable. They apply to most situations. However, a number of job-specific skills are also transferable. If you can operate a drill press, you have skills to operate other types of machinery. If you can balance a personal bank account, you have math aptitude skills to balance a business account. If you coordinate events, lead meetings, participate on teams for community activities or personal interests, you have skills that transfer to employment.

Transferable skills are important for many reasons. Many job seekers are unlikely to find a job identical to their previous employment. Therefore, it is critical for them to carefully evaluate how their skills transfer into other opportunities.

People seeking their first job, making a major career change, or returning to employment after a long absence will mostly use transferable skills in their job search.

Skill Identification Methods

There are many methods for identifying skills. Whatever method you use, consider the following:

- Don't get hung up over definitions or the process of how you identify your skills. The goal is to generate a list of skills. Definitions and process are simply tools to help you achieve that goal.
- Don't limit yourself. Give yourself the benefit of the doubt. List everything that remotely looks like a skill.
- You do not have to be an expert to claim a skill. Include skills you may be just learning.

Have fun! Make a game out of it. Work through your skill identification with a friend.

Skills Identification

Method

Step 1: Write the title of an employment-related activity. Focus on those activities that potentially demonstrate skill and experience relative to employment. You may get these titles from skills you may have gained while working for community organizations, volunteer activities, and employment.

Step 2: List the tasks involved in performing this activity. Tasks are the basic functions of an activity.

Step 3: List the skills involved in accomplishing each task. Be sure to include job, self-management, and transferable skills.

Method

Look for skill words that you recognize in books, magazines, publications, and on the Internet. Skill words can be found in: The Occupational Outlook Handbook (may be found at your local library or Minnesota WorkForce Center), how-to books, hobby books, technical manuals, newspapers, magazines, and classified advertisements.

Method

Network with friends, associates, and family. Ask them what skills they see that you have.

The main reason some people have trouble finding a job is:

Failure to Describe Skills or Abilities Clearly

Activity Title	Task	Skills— job, self-management, transferable
Administrative Assistant	Answering company correspondence	Typing, word processing, tactfulness, timeliness, responsible, creative, dependable, detail-oriented, sincere, tactful, meeting deadlines, communicating, helping others, problem solving, checking for accuracy, researching, writing clearly and concisely
	Answering telephones	Getting along well with others, listening, mediating, communicating, respectful, helpful, resolving conflict, developing rapport, assertiveness, dependable, outgoing, pleasant, sensitive, tolerant, detail-oriented, enthusiastic, friendly, intelligent, kind, mature, patient, sincere, tactful, understanding

Skills Identification

GOAL SETTING

Career Planning

During the average lifetime, an adult will have many jobs, several different careers, and will spend half their waking hours working. Yet that same person will spend more time watching television in one week than they will spend in their lifetime planning for employment!

Employment is more than a job. It shapes a big part of your life and deserves consideration. With the frequency that people change careers, it also deserves reconsideration throughout your work life. Career planning is a vast topic which will not be covered. If you have not planned your career, you are encouraged to do so now. Career counselors are available through Minnesota WorkForce Centers, schools, employment service providers, and private organizations. There are many books on career planning available through the library or local bookstores.

The Mature Worker

As a mature worker, you have achieved many of your career objectives. Mature workers have multiple skills they have learned through their participation in the workforce and through the volunteering they may have done.

You are in charge of your career. You have adapted to many changes and now you can use this to your advantage. Mature workers bring to the job many assets that younger people have not yet acquired. You are reliable and have experience, multiple skills, and a strong work ethic!

Mature workers often hear the phrases: "you are overqualified" or "you wouldn't be interested in this job." You must identify the benefits you bring to the workforce, thus making you the best candidate.

Job Search Objective

You must have a job goal to conduct an effective job search campaign. You cannot set out on a quest for employment looking for just anything. If you do, you will waste a lot of effort. Employers will quickly recognize that you do not know what you want. This is comparable to a salesperson trying to sell a product without knowing its features. Salespeople know what their product can do and they know the market for their product. In the same manner, you need to target your job search campaign to those employers who need your skills and can offer you the opportunities you are seeking.

Simply saying that you are looking for a good job that pays well is not enough. Identifying the specific types of jobs for which you are qualified will focus your effort to those employers who match your employment objective. Furthermore, when you approach an employer, describe your skills which will tell them what it is you can do. Tell them the kind of work you are looking for. Do not expect them to analyze your qualifications and tell you where you might fit into their organization. Skills sell the product— you!

Take the time to think about what you want from that next job. Conditions of employment, wages, location, hours, and benefits are important considerations. You may also be looking for job security or advancement potential.

Judy lived in a small town in Minnesota. She went to college and became a certified art therapist. Full of hope, she pursued her dream. However, she never worked as an art therapist. There simply are not many such jobs in small communities and she didn't want to move. Her job goal was not achievable because of her location requirement.

Skills Identification

Jim was an experienced tool and die maker who was laid off due to a plant closing. He was considered one of the best in his trade and was at the upper end of the pay scale. After investing six months in an exhaustive job search with no success, Jim was forced to reconsider his goals. His question was whether he should lower his expectations or expand the commutable distance he was willing to travel. His decision was to expand the distance, and within a short time he secured employment that met his standards.

Bob had extensive experience making ceramic figures. He mixed materials and extruded them into molds. Once the piece was set, it was then sanded and inspected. Since most ceramic companies are small, Bob was challenged to find opportunities that used his skills. Bob discovered the same basic extruding and finishing operations are used to work with plastics, light metals, and even heavy foundry work.

After a long absence to raise her three children, Sue reentered employment. She had no recent employment experience, and her education is outdated. However, Sue has mastered many skills through managing a household on a limited budget and through volunteer work with the YWCA. Through a careful skill assessment and some creativity, Sue was able to identify many skills important to potential employers.

Look for ways to expand your opportunities. This means you may have to make some choices. Goals should be realistic and achievable. Keep this in mind when considering your expectations. A good strategy is to write down all the conditions that you would like in a job, then categorize them as "required," "desired," and "optional." If you find that you are not getting interviews, or that you are not finding jobs that meet your expectations, reevaluate your criteria for employment.

Transferable Skills and Your Job Search Goal

Transferable skills are another way to expand your job search. Once you have identified your skills, look for ways they might transfer to other jobs. The transferability of self-management skills is obvious. All employers are looking for motivation and dependability. But many job skills are also transferable, and transferable job skills open doors to new opportunities.

Look for ways that your skills transfer to other employment opportunities. If you decide to pursue these opportunities, your next challenge is to find effective ways to present these skills to a potential employer.

Goal setting is an important part of a successful job search. It is critical that you take the time to establish clear job search goals. This takes research and an honest self-assessment. Consider talking to a professional career counselor and taking career tests (aptitude, interest, values, and personality inventory). You will certainly want to research the labor market.

Focus on the job that you plan to pursue right now. Your immediate need for employment should be a step in your long-term career plans.

As you explore your job search goal, you will be considering criteria for the ultimate job. You will be reaching for the best. Throughout the process, a healthy dose of reality is important. Remember that your goals must be attainable. If you find your dream job is not immediately achievable, re-evaluate and plan the steps to achieve your goal. Secondary job goals are often among these steps. A secondary goal may include part-time, temporary, evening, or contract employment. It may be an opportunity for advancement or self-employment. It may be short-term employment while you pursue other opportunities. Whatever the case, consider secondary goals early in your job search.

The worksheets and checklists at the end of this chapter will help you explore your values and establish your employment goals. Another useful activity is to return to the list of your skills and mark those that you would (and those you would not) like to use in future employment.

You can only hit a target if you aim for it.

Skills Identification

THE EMPLOYER PERSPECTIVE

Generally, employers are not in the business of career development. Although many employers are interested in the career goals of their employees, the needs of the organization are their first priority. For a successful job search, match your skills and goals to the needs of the employer.

You do not have to match all of the skills needed for an occupation to pursue that occupation. The best candidates for a job rarely match all of the requirements of an employer. Many factors go into the hiring process—including personality and motivation. The most successful job seekers may not be the most qualified. Those who demonstrate the desired qualities sought by employers are the ones who will ultimately succeed.

Strategies for identifying the skills employers desire are similar to those for identifying your own skills. The goal is to learn as much as possible about the industry, occupation, and employer. Position descriptions, industry and company literature, employment advertisements, and Internet websites are all sources of information. You may also draw on the knowledge of your contacts, conduct informational interviews, or participate in Internet discussion groups.

Rita is considering retail sales as an immediate job goal. Her research shows that retail employers require good customer service skills. Customer service is not a skill that she identified. Her past employment as an inventory clerk in a warehouse required little customer contact. Yet, in that job she coordinated the distribution of inventory to several departments and worked very closely with staff. This work experience, along with her volunteer experience as a school fund raiser, demonstrates excellent customer service skills.

Conclusion

This chapter has focused on the need to identify your skills, set job search goals, and match it to the needs of potential employers. Once you accomplish this, you will be ready to begin your job search. These efforts are important to job search success. They will help you organize your job search, write resumes, complete applications, interview, and negotiate the best job offer.

The important thing is not where you are, but where you are going.

Skills Identification

ADDENDUM

Accomplishment Worksheet

An effective salesperson will describe the specifications of a product as well as promote its performance and note examples of success and customer satisfaction. Your accomplishments are a record of success. Employers want to know how, where, and when you used those skills. They want to hear how you excelled in your performance. Your accomplishments set you apart from the competition.

List your accomplishments on the blanks below. Include any success in your life. There are no wrong answers. Include some accomplishments from past employment or an employment-related activity. Include ways you improved, met a specific challenge, or saved time and money. These may have been from your own effort or as part of a team. When stating an accomplishment, use measures whenever possible. Examples:

"Successfully managed $500,000 accounts receivables and reduced delinquent accounts by 15 percent."

"Participated on a fund-raising team for the YWCA which raised $15,000 for youth programs."

"Successfully managed a household of four on a $900 a month budget."

"Restored a 1936 Ford to original condition."

Accomplishments

_____
_____
_____
_____
_____
_____
_____
_____
_____
_____
_____
_____
_____
_____
_____
_____
_____
_____
_____
_____
_____

Skills Identification

How Others See Me

Ask someone who is close to you— spouse, sibling, roommate or friend— to circle 10 to 15 traits that describe you. Their impressions may surprise you and possibly point you in some new direction. Look for ways to maximize your strengths and overcome your weaknesses.

able	foolish	mature	realistic
active	frank	modest	reasonable
accepting	friendly	mystical	reassuring
adaptable	frugal	naive	reflective
ambitious	gentle	negative	relaxed
anxious	giving	neurotic	reliable
assertive	gruff	noisy	religious
bitter	gullible	observant	remote
bold	hard	obsessive	resentful
bright	helpful	organized	reserved
calm	helpless	original	resolute
careless	honorable	overconfident	respectful
caring	idealistic	overemotional	responsible
certain	imaginative	overprotective	responsive
cheerful	inconsiderate	passive	rigid
clever	independent	paternal	sarcastic
cold	innovative	patient	satisfied
confident	insensitive	perceptive	scientific
conforming	insincere	perfectionist	searching
controlled	intelligent	persuasive	self-accepting
courageous	introverted	petty	self-assertive
critical	intuitive	playful	self-aware
cynical	irresponsible	pleasant	self-conscious
demanding	irritable	pompous	self-indulgent
dependable	jealous	powerful	self-righteous
dependent	jovial	precise	unpredictable
determined	juvenile	pretentious	unreasonable
dignified	kind	principled	unstructured
disciplined	knowledgeable	progressive	useful
domineering	lazy	protective	vain
dutiful	liberal	proud	vulnerable
efficient	lively	quarrelsome	warm
elusive	logical	questioning	wise
ethical	loving	quiet	withdrawn
extroverted	manipulative	radical	witty
fair	materialistic	rational	worried
fearful	maternal	reactionary	youthful

Skills Identification

Occupational Titles

Use the following list of job titles as a brainstorming tool when considering job goals.

Accountant	Doctor	Manager
Architect	Drafter	Mason
Assembler	Editor	Nurse
Cabinet Maker	Engineer	Painter
Carpenter	Financial Analyst	Programmer
Cashier	Graphic Designer	Sales
Chef	Inspector	Scientist
Clerk	Lab Technician	Secretary
Cook	Librarian	Teacher
Counselor	Machine Operator	Veterinarian
Dentist	Machinist	Welder

Employment-Related Titles

Community involvement and volunteer experience may be a valuable resource for your job search. The following are common titles. Just attach the name of the activity or community organization.

Campaigner	Fund Raiser	Promoter	Teacher
Consultant	Leader	Secretary	Treasurer
Coordinator	Member	Solicitor	Volunteer
Director	Organizer	Sponsor	Worker

Example: YMCA **Volunteer** or School **Fund Raiser**.

Skills Identification

Job Skills

The following is a short list of job skills. (There are literally thousands of job specific skills.) You will have to research the job skills specific to your occupation.

Accounting	Cooking	Filing	Public Speaking
Auditing	Counseling	Hammering	Scheduling
Brake alignments	Customer Service	Interviewing	Soldering
Building Maintenance	Desktop Publishing	Keyboarding	Teaching
C++ Programming	Detailing	LAN Administration	Technical Writing
Carpet Laying	Drill Press Operation	Management	Telemarketing
Cleaning	Driving	Mechanical Drafting	Typing
CNC Machine Operation	Editing	Metal Fabrication	Welding
Composite Engineering	Electronic Repair	Payroll Accounting	Writing

Computer Software: Auto CAD, Excel, Lotus, MicrosoftWord, PageMaker, WordPerfect

Self-Management Skills

You use self-management skills every day to survive and get along. Self-management skills are important because employers hire people who will "fit in" with the work group. Circle the self-management skills you possess right now.

Critical Skills:
- Follow instructions
- Get along well with others
- Get things done
- Honest
- Punctual
- Responsible

Adaptive Skills:
- Assertive
- Assume Responsibility
- Competitive
- Complete assignments
- Creative
- Decisive
- Dependable
- Detail-oriented
- Diplomatic
- Enthusiastic
- Flexible
- Friendly
- Highly motivated
- Ingenious
- Integrity
- Intelligent
- Inventive
- Kind
- Learn quickly
- Mature
- Open Minded
- Outgoing
- Patient
- Persistent
- Physically strong
- Pleasant
- Proud of doing a good job
- Results-oriented
- Self-motivated
- Sense of direction (purpose)
- Sense of humor
- Sensitive
- Sincere
- Sociable
- Tactful
- Tolerant
- Tough
- Trusting
- Understanding
- Willing to learn new things

CREATIVE Job Search

Skills Identification

Transferable Skills

Transferable skills can be transferred from one job, or even one career to another.

Critical Transferable Skills may get you higher levels of responsibility and pay. Emphasize them in an interview as well as on your resume.

Critical Transferable Skills:

- Accept responsibility
- Budgeting
- Efficiency
- Meet deadlines
- Project planning
- Public speaking
- Sales
- Supervise others

"Thing" Skills:

- Assembling
- Balancing, juggling
- Counting
- Drawing, painting
- Driving
- Endurance
- Finishing/refinishing
- Gathering
- Grinding
- Hammering
- Hand crafts
- Keyboarding, typing
- Keypunching, drilling
- Manual dexterity
- Modeling, remodeling
- Observing/inspecting
- Operating machines
- Physical agility, strength
- Precise, tolerance, standards
- Restoring
- Sandblasting
- Sewing
- Sorting
- Weaving

"People" Skills:

- Caring
- Comforting
- Communicating
- Conflict management
- Conflict resolution
- Counseling
- Consulting
- Developing rapport
- Diplomacy
- Diversity
- Empathy
- Encouraging
- Group facilitating
- Helping others
- Inspiring trust
- Inquiry
- Instructing
- Interviewing
- Listening
- Mediating
- Mentoring
- Motivating
- Negotiating
- Outgoing
- Problem solving
- Respect
- Responsive
- Sensitive
- Sympathy
- Tolerance

CREATIVE Job Search

Skills Identification

Transferable Skills

Dealing with data:

Analyzing	Cost analysis	Investigating
Auditing	Counting	Interrelate
Averaging	Detail-oriented	Organizing
Budgeting	Evaluating	Problem solving
Calculating/computing	Examining	Recording facts
Checking for accuracy	Financial or fiscal analysis	Research
Classifying	Financial management	Surveying
Comparing	Financial records	Synthesizing
Compiling	Following instructions	Taking inventory

Using words, ideas:

Advertising	Imaginative	Quick thinking
Articulate	Inventive	Sign language
Brainstorming	Logical	Speech writing
Correspondence	Promotional writing	Telephone skills
Design	Public speaking	Write clearly, concisely
Edit	Publicity	Verbal communication

Leadership:

Competitive	Integrity	Risk taker
Coordinating	Judgment	Run meetings
Decision-making	Manage, direct others	Self-confident
Decisive	Mediate problems	Self-directed
Delegate	Motivate people	Self-motivated
Direct others	Multi-tasking	Sets an example, sets pace
Evaluation	Negotiate agreements	Solve problems
Goal setting	Organization	Strategic planning
Influence others	Planning	Supervision
Initiate new tasks	Results-oriented	Work schedules

Creative, Artistic:

Artistic	Illustrating, sketching	Poetic images
Dance, body movement	Mechanical drawing	Present artistic ideas
Designing	Model-making	Rendering
Drawing, painting	Perform	Singing
Expressive	Photography	Visualize shapes
Handicrafts	Playing a musical instrument	Visualizing

Skills Identification

Values Checklist

Work-related values are a part of setting job search goals. Decide what working conditions are important to you.

Instructions

1. Check the box next to those conditions that you would like in a job. Add additional values on the blanks.
2. Draw a line through those conditions that you would not like in a job.

☐ Authority	☐ Other benefits	☐ Travel
☐ Career enhancement	☐ Pace, fast or slow	☐ Variety
☐ Casual environment	☐ Position	☐ Wage
☐ Challenge	☐ Power	☐ Work indoors/outdoors
☐ Close supervision	☐ Public transportation	☐ Work on a team
☐ Commuting distance	☐ Public contact	☐ Work alone
☐ Competence	☐ Quality environment	☐ Work under pressure
☐ Creativity	☐ Recognition	☐ _____
☐ Decision-making	☐ Regular work week	☐ _____
☐ Diversity	☐ Relocation	☐ _____
☐ Excitement	☐ Respect	☐ _____
☐ Flexible schedule	☐ Retirement benefits	☐ _____
☐ Formal environment	☐ Security	☐ _____
☐ Health benefits	☐ Shift work	☐ _____
☐ Independence	☐ Size of company (large, small)	☐ _____
☐ Learning opportunities	☐ Skill Building (training)	☐ _____
☐ Organizational structure	☐ Status	☐ _____

Skills Identification
Goal Worksheet

Instructions

1. Write the occupational title of your immediate job goal representing the kind of jobs you plan to pursue right now. If you have more than one distinct job goal, complete this exercise for each one. See page 43 for a list of "Occupational Titles". Review the values that you identified as important to your job goals on the "Values Checklist" on page 47. Which conditions do you require in a new opportunity? Which conditions do you desire?

2. Write your required values and desired values from the "Values Checklist" in the appropriate space below.

3. Evaluate whether or not your expectations are reasonable and attainable. To accomplish this, conduct labor market research (page 28).

1. Job Goal
   _____
   _____
   _____
   _____
   _____
   _____

2. Required values
   _____
   _____
   _____
   _____
   _____
   _____
   _____

3. Desired values
   _____
   _____
   _____
   _____
   _____
   _____
   _____

4. Reality check: Are these expectations reasonable and attainable?

   Yes ☐   No ☐

   <u>If you answered "no" or are unsure,
   re-evaluate your values.</u>

CREATIVE Job Search 48

Skills Identification

NOTES

Networking

30 People — A. People who return my phone call
　　　　　　　Friends, Parents, Family, Neighbors
　　　　Tell the kind of Job looking for

60　B. Referrals

120　C. Referrals of Referrals

Skills Identification

NOTES

Resumes and Cover Letters

Review of qualifications
Essential information only
Skills based
Unique – what makes you special
Marketing a product – You!
Effective – gets you noticed

Resumes and Cover Letters

Your resume should be an honest presentation of your best qualities.

Much preparation goes into an excellent resume and cover letter. You do not simply begin by writing. First establish clear goals for your job search. Then identify your skills that match your goals. You need to gather supporting materials and summarize your past employment-related experiences. Finally, you will write, rewrite, and edit until the resume is perfect. Always have someone proofread your resume. You may want someone to repeat back to you what your resume says. Continuously work at keeping your perfect resume up-to-date. As you grow, your resume should grow with you; its development should mirror your personal and professional development.

Do not overwhelm employers by providing more information than necessary. Do not try to be everything to everyone. The greatest challenge will not be what to include in your resume, but what to leave out. An attention-getting resume must be targeted, to the point, and must clearly identify your qualifications. Focus on skills and accomplishments with specific attention to actual results. Hobbies, crafts, and clubs can also give you accomplishments and skills.

You are not ready to approach prospective employers until you have taken these steps. Since it has to be done anyway, there is no better time than the present. If you are already engaged in these activities, you are that much closer to a finished product.

Skill Identification

Employers want to know what you can do, not just where you have worked. If you cannot clearly state at least 20 skills directly associated with your job goal, you are not ready to write your resume.

Take the time to work on developing a list of your skills. As you develop your list, identify examples of places where you have used your skills. Employment-related skills do not always come from employment. They may originate from education, volunteer work, personal interests, and life experiences. Be very specific when describing your skills. Also, be sure to state your skills in a positive light. Avoid any language that may reduce their value. Always be honest and positive.

When drafting your resume, clearly identify your skills. There are several formats that can be used, but your skills should stand out. Whenever possible, state your skills as expert skills, to avoid being perceived as a generalist. As an example, if you have word processing skills, state which software packages you have used. All resumes today need to be skill-based resumes. Whatever style or format you use, your resume must clearly communicate the skills you bring to the job.

Goal Setting

An important element in resume preparation is establishing clear goals or objectives. It is critical that you target your resume to a specific occupational goal. The content of your resume should point to that goal. Without this focus, your resume will be mediocre at best. Great resumes are ones in which every piece of information points to a clear occupational objective. If you have already established specific goals, you are prepared to write your resume. If not, you are encouraged to first spend some time establishing your goals.

As you write your resume, keep your goal in view. This will help you decide what to include, what to leave out, and will help target your resume. One strategy is to write your goal on a separate piece of paper and weigh each item in your resume against your goal. If it is not clear how the item relates to your goal, then strongly consider eliminating it. (See the Skills Identification chapter on page 38 for information on goals.)

Resumes must be skill-based and clearly target your objectives and the needs of employers.

Resumes and Cover Letters

The Language of Resumes

Resumes must be skill-based and clearly target your objectives and the needs of employers. Beyond this, there are many ways to present these skills. You may use narrative, bullets, lists of keywords, highlights, or other presentation styles. The resume must have impact and flair. What you say is important, but how you say it is just as important. An excellent method is to use action verbs to highlight your qualifications. It is one thing to say that you have a particular skill; it is another to proclaim that you have excelled in its performance. "Mastered three word processing programs: WordPerfect, Microsoft Word, and AmiPro." "Successfully increased regional sales by 1.2 million." "Organized a neighborhood block party of 50 homes, which helped to reduce crime by 15 percent." "Achieved 100 percent attendance during training." Notice the use of measures to strengthen the statement. Look for similar measures to complement your resume. There are "sample action verbs" on page 55.

Resumes are not literary; they are promotional. The rules of grammar are modified from formal writing. Complete sentences are not necessary. Avoid the use of "I," as the subject of the resume is assumed to be the person named in the heading of the resume. Avoid long narratives and use lots of bullets and key phrases. Someone looking at the resume should be able to figure out the content without reading the details. The resume should draw the reader's attention and create a desire to know more. The goal is to win an interview. It is at the interview that the job is won. The resume is like a preview of coming attractions; you want to save the best for the presentation. Therefore, it is best if the resume creates questions in the mind of the reader. These questions should not cast doubt on your qualifications or integrity, but create a desire to know more about you. "Profitably managed up to $500,000 accounts receivable, reducing delinquent accounts from 22.7 percent to 10.4 percent," is just such a statement. You can also use life experience, such as "Organized a group of 50 community members that raised over $75,000 for playground equipment" or "Managed and led a scout troop of 25 that completed 15 community service projects." Those statements should prompt an employer to find out more about you.

> It is one thing to say that you have a particular skill; it is another to proclaim that you have excelled in its performance.

Resumes and Cover Letters

RESUME FORMATS

There are three common resume formats: chronological, functional, and combination. By using the Resume Comparison Chart on page 56, you can determine which format and variation will best display your strengths. Your career objectives will also influence your choice. Another way to select the best format is to complete the "Resume Worksheets". (See sample resumes later in the chapter.)

Chronological

The emphasis for this format is on a chronological listing of employment and employment-related experiences. The format highlights the recent employment, while de-emphasizing experiences further back in time. The chronological resume is for those with a consistent employment history, no gaps in employment, and whose past employment experiences are directly related to their current employment goals. A steady work record with increasing responsibilities can be effectively showcased using this format. You would begin by listing your most recent employment experiences and working backward. Include dates, names, and contact information such as addresses and phone numbers. This may NOT be the best format for individuals with job gaps, new graduates, or a person changing careers.

When listing your experience, chronicle five to ten years of employment history. Experiences over ten years ago begin to lose impact and open the potential for age discrimination. If you have valuable experience beyond ten years, there are ways to present it other than chronologically. Read the following on Functional and Combination resume formats.

Functional

The functional resume highlights skills, experience, and accomplishments without identifying specific dates, names, and places. In this format, information is organized by functions or skills, advertising the specific qualifications needed for the occupation. This format works very well for people changing careers, including military personnel moving into civilian employment. It is also effective for first-time job seekers, those reentering the workforce after a gap in employment, and people who want to emphasize experience that may be viewed as outdated. In a true functional resume there is no chronological listing of employment. Consequently, many employers do not like this format; it creates suspicion that the person may be trying to hide something. The employer may suspect a job hopper, an older applicant trying to disguise age, a lack of career progression, underemployment, employment gaps, or too little relevant experience.

Combination

The combination resume brings the best of both the chronological and functional resumes. It features a functional section that highlights skills, accomplishments, and experience. It also includes a chronological listing of employment, education, and employment-related experiences. The combination resume is a very effective format for many job seekers. The best chronological resume can be enhanced with a section highlighting skills, accomplishments, and experience. The functional resume can be strengthened with a chronological listing of employment experiences.

Resumes and Cover Letters

RESUME VARIATIONS

Keyword

The keyword resume is a variation that adds a listing of skills to the beginning of any standard resume format. Critical occupational skills placed at the beginning add impact to the resume and help capture the reader's attention. This variation is effective for all career fields and skill levels. It is a very effective strategy for creating scannable resumes. The format for a keyword resume would look something like this:

```
                Name
               Address
                Phone
         Employment Objective

         Summary of Skills
            (Keyword List)
     Skill      Skill      Skill
     Skill      Skill      Skill
     Skill      Skill      Skill

             Resume Body
  (Chronological, Functional, or Combination)
  _____
  _____
```

Samples of Occupational Keywords

Account Management	Ecology	Personal Computer
Accounts Receivable	Electronics	Process Metallurgy
Acquisitions	Employee Assistance	Proposal Writing
Bachelor's Degree	Engineer	Psychology
Bank Card	Equipment Vendor	Public Relations
Bank Reconciliation	Facilitator	Purchasing
Batch Processing	Financial Planning	Radio
Benchmarking	Food Preparation	Raw Materials
Blueprint Reading	Gas Pipeline	Receptionist
Brochures	Goal Setting	Reporter
Budget	Graphic Design	Research
Bulletins	Guest Services	Sales
CAD	Harnessing	Secretarial
Calibrator	Hiring/Firing	Software Modeling
Carpentry	Hotel	Spanish
Cash Flow	ISO 9000	Spreadsheets
Cell Culture Media	Journalism	Statistical Process Control
Cement	Journeyman	Stick Welding
Child Care	Layout Design	Strategic Planning
Claims Adjudication	Logic Analyzer	Student Personnel
Commercial Leasing	Magnetic Theory	Supervisor
Copy Editing	Manager	Taxonomy
Counselor	Mapping	Teacher
Crisis Management	Marketing	Technical Writing
Cross-Cultural Training	Master's Degree	Time Management
Debugging	Microprocessor	Transportation
Decision Making	Microsoft Word	Travel
Demographics	Nursing	Wave Solder
Dental Management	Oscillator	WordPerfect
Die Casting	Patient Advocate	Workflow
Dietitian	Payroll	Writer
Drywall	Pelletizing	

Occupational keywords include skills, titles, degrees, and occupational buzz words.

Resumes and Cover Letters

Targeted

More of a method than a style, the targeted resume directs skills and experience to the specific needs of one employer. All resumes should target the needs of a specific occupation. In addition, this approach targets the specific needs of an employer and a specific job. It requires careful research of the employer's needs. Sources for information include position descriptions, employer profiles, industry publications, networking, and informational interviews. When drafting a targeted resume, direct your skills and experience to the specific needs of the employer by typing some of their keywords into your resume. This is a very powerful resume strategy that can set you apart from the competition and capture an employer's interest. For executive positions and specialized technical jobs, this strategy is almost a necessity.

Convenient access to a computer and word processing skills will help to make this method work. Using the combination format, set up a resume template with header information and the chronological summary of your employment. Then customize the functional section of the resume, the summary of skills, accomplishments, and qualifications to meet the needs of a specific employer. Be sure to name your objective with the exact job title.

Sample List of Action Verbs

Achieved	Created	Formulated	Recruited
Administered	Decided	Founded	Rectified
Affected	Defined	Generated	Researched
Analyzed	Delegated	Governed	Reviewed
Applied	Designed	Grouped	Revised
Appraised	Detailed	Guided	Scheduled
Approved	Developed	Handled	Searched
Arranged	Directed	Illustrated	Secured
Assessed	Distributed	Implemented	Selected
Attained	Earned	Improved	Simplified
Awarded	Effected	Increased	Sold
Built	Encouraged	Influenced	Solved
Calculated	Enforced	Initiated	Stimulated
Catalogued	Enlarged	Inspired	Structured
Clarified	Equipped	Installed	Succeeded
Coached	Established	Instituted	Summarized
Compared	Estimated	Integrated	Supported
Composed	Evaluated	Interviewed	Tailored
Conceived	Examined	Introduced	Taught
Conducted	Excelled	Invented	Transformed
Constructed	Executed	Investigated	Translated
Contracted	Expanded	Launched	United
Controlled	Experimented	Maintained	Validated
Convinced	Facilitated	Mastered	Verified
Correlated	Formed	Recorded	

How you say it is just as important as what you say. Use action words to stress performance, motivation, and a passion for excellence. Use a dictionary, thesaurus, or job descriptions for more words.

Resumes and Cover Letters

Resume Comparison Chart

Format		Characteristic	Advantage	Disadvantage	Use	Don't Use If
	Chronological	Presents information in reverse order, most recent experience listed first. Offers concise picture of you as a potential employee	Easy to write. Emphasizes steady employment record. Format is familiar	Calls attention to employment gaps. Skills are difficult to spot unless they are listed in the most recent job	To emphasize past career growth and development. When continuing in the same career. When the name of former employer may be significant to prospective employer	There are gaps in your work history. Calling attention to your age could be a problem. You have changed jobs often. Entering job market for first time or after a long absence
	Functional	Focuses on specific strengths and skills important to employers	Brief and well-structured. Focus on skills, not history. De-emphasizes a spotty work history	No detailed work history. Content may appear to lack depth	When entering the job market or when reentering after a long absence. When work experience has been varied or unrelated. When changing careers. When primarily consulting or doing freelance work	Want to emphasize growth or development. Responsibilities and functions in recent jobs were limited
	Combination	All the flexibility and strength of the functional and chronological combined	Shows off a strong employment record with upward mobility. Showcases relevant skills and abilities and supportive employment record. Emphasizes transferable skills	Work history is often on the second page and employer may not read that far	When shorter functional format would be too sketchy. To offer a complete picture of abilities and work history	Experience is limited. There are wide gaps in work history
Variations (Format)	Keyword	Allows for focused resumes that target skills	Skills are listed briefly and at the beginning of the resume. Easy for employer to scan and find skills	May be redundant information to include keywords at the top of your resume. Still an unfamiliar format to many employers	For all scannable systems of job screening. For all new graduates, those reentering the work place or changing careers	There is rarely a time you cannot use this variation. It can be used in combination with any or all of the other formats
	Targeted	Highly focused document aimed at a particular job. A "capsule" of work experience	Brief and direct. Easy to read	May focus too tightly on one particular job. Content may appear sparse	When job target is specific. When you need separate resumes for different career paths	You are not prepared to put the effort into writing an excellent resume

CREATIVE Job Search

BASIC PRINCIPLES OF RESUME WRITING

Keep it brief!

Your resume is an overview of your qualifications— not your life story. It is a "preview of coming attractions" which creates the desire to see the rest of the show. One to two pages is the standard for a resume read by the human eye, and up to three pages for a scannable resume. If your resume is more than one page, the first page must capture the reader's attention. If it fails to do so, the remaining pages will not be read.

Focus

Don't try to be everything to everyone. Target your job search and your resume to your specific occupational goals.

Multiple Resumes

Generally, you should concentrate first on one well-written resume that targets your immediate job search. Make sure this resume represents you well to a wide range of employers, and is suitable for scanning. If you have more than one objective, additional resumes may be required. For example, if you are planning to pursue two distinct occupations such as realtor and bookkeeper, you would need two resumes. If you only use the targeted resume approach, you would also write a unique resume to each employer.

Visual Impact

A piece of sales literature has only about two seconds to attract the reader's attention. Similarly, the resume must attract the employer even before it is read. Many advertising techniques apply, including the use of white space, bullets, indentation, and varied type style. Professional printing produces a high quality product, but can be expensive. Laser quality printing is an excellent alternative. Never handwrite your resume! Make sure there are no typographical, grammatical, or spelling errors. Ask someone to proofread your resume to help eliminate errors.

Insure Integrity

Your resume is specifically designed to paint the best picture possible of you. Place the emphasis on the positive, not the negative. It should be an honest statement of your best qualities. Your resume should hold up under scrutiny. Facts and numbers must be believable. The content of the resume should be in harmony. Dates should be consistent while experience and related activities should support your qualifications.

Scannable Resumes

Many employers and employment agencies are using electronic resume scanning systems to screen resumes, a trend that will increase in the future. When writing any resume, consider its scannability. Generally, there is little difference between a good scannable resume and one that is effective for the human eye. Ultimately, all resumes will be looked at by a person, so your resume must work for both.

Overqualified

If you consistently hear that you are overqualified or are concerned that you will be perceived as such, then you have not effectively targeted your resume. When writing your resume, target it to the level of employment and to the occupation or employer. If you are pursuing more than one distinct level of employment, then consider a separate resume for each. Present the information that you believe is important. You don't have to tell everything. If you have an advanced degree in a field unrelated to your goal, leave it off.

Resumes and Cover Letters

Resume Content

Name Block

Use your full first name. Avoid using nicknames. If you have a preference to be called by a shortened version of your full name, it is acceptable to put this name in parentheses or quotes (Elizabeth— prefer to be called "Betty"). Your address should not contain abbreviations. Your phone number should include the area code. Provide a phone number where you can be reached at all times, either by an answering machine or an alternate message number. Do not put your name and address on one line for a scannable resume, as the computer may be confused by this format. Type your name in bold and/or all capitals to make it stand out.

ELIZABETH "BETTY" APPLICANT

1443 Hire Me Lane
Employability, Minnesota 55555

(555) 555-5555

Employment or Career Objective

Include an objective when you are pursuing a specific job goal, or when you know the exact title of the position you are applying for. The objective targets your resume, but also limits its use to those jobs that match your goal. Objectives may be considered optional on your resume. You can also use a short summary of your skills and qualifications. If your objective is not included in your resume, state it in your cover letter.

Summary Statements

The summary or qualification statement documents your work experience, achievement, and skills. This statement is a summary of the experience and qualifications that are the most pertinent to the job for which you are applying. This is recommended for all job seekers as a way to get the employer's attention. The summary should be three or four lines or a series of phrases that may be used in place of the employment objective or just following it.

To be effective, the summary or qualification statement must indicate that you are qualified for the position you are seeking. It is often read first, and if it catches the reader's attention, chances are, the rest of the resume will be read. Summary example: "Resourceful Planner/Coordinator with extensive knowledge of inventory control and on-line inventory systems. Recognized by management for innovation and initiative in implementing JIT techniques, as well as interdepartmental communications and supervisory skills."

Employment History

List your most recent employment first. A general standard is to list the last three jobs, or the last ten years, whichever comes first. Focus on recent jobs and those that are most appropriate to your goals. If you have large gaps in employment or have changed jobs frequently, consider using a functional resume. How you use your resume and the make-up of your experience will determine the amount of information to include. Many job seekers and employers use the resume as a substitute application (this is very useful if the application works against your qualifications). As a substitute application, the resume should include employer contact information. Many resumes list employer name, city, and state. Contact information is provided through an employment application or reference sheet. One advantage in limiting this information is to keep the resume focused on your qualifications. Also, some people may not want a prospective employer to be able to easily reach a previous employer. The choice is yours. There is no one standard that fits all situations.

Organizations

List organizational memberships related to your job goal. Avoid using non-employer related or controversial organizations. Avoid mentioning specific religious or political affiliations, or other potentially controversial groups unless they directly relate to the job you want.

Education

If your skills and experience come from employment, list employment first and education last. List education first if the emphasis is on education (a recent graduate). If you are a college graduate, state the name of the institution, location (city and state), degree earned, and field of study.

Resumes and Cover Letters

Additional Points to Consider Regarding Education

- Carefully consider listing the dates you graduated from school. List recent education dates because it increases its value. Older educational experiences may not be valued by the reader and may be used in age discrimination.

- Do not list high school graduation if you have completed a college degree. If you have taken post-high school classes but did not achieve a degree, list your high school.

- When listing recent education, target specific skills and academic accomplishments.

- A GED can be listed as a high school graduate. If the GED was achieved through a local school, list the name of that school. Otherwise, leave off the name of the school. You may choose to list the last school attended or the school district name.

- Do not include an education section if you dropped out of high school and had no formal training either in school or from an employer.

- Include relevant employer-sponsored training. Be sure that the training is targeted to your job goal. Summarize extensive employer training by type and only include training that is relevant to a new job.

- If you have conducted a thorough independent study into a job-related topic, you may summarize it as part of your education.

- If you are currently taking classes or pursuing a degree related to your job goal, include that information. List the skills acquired, academic accomplishments, and the projected date of completion.

Military

Include military experience that fills gaps in employment or supports your job goal as part of your work history. "Civilianize" your military language so your skills and experience match the employer's needs. For example, change a truck vehicle mechanic to light diesel mechanic; logistics to warehouse or material inventory control; war college to advanced training; chief petty officer to supervisor or lead worker; or NCOIC to supervisor.

Hobbies/Personal Interests

Include hobbies/personal interests if they are employment-related, not controversial, and they show skill and experience.

Include hobbies if they are employment-related and show skill and experience.

References

Do not include references on the resume. Do not use "References available upon request." It is assumed by employers that you will provide this information. Once an employer requests references, be prepared to give them three to five references who can speak about your work habits and professional employment qualifications. Always seek permission before using someone as a reference.

Awards or Recognition

Let the employer know of any awards or recognition you have received (employee of the month, etc.), if it is timely and appropriate.

59 CREATIVE Job Search

Resumes and Cover Letters

Tips for Scannable and Readable Resumes

- Give priority to the skills on your resume. Employers want to know what you can do, not just where you have been. This is why scannable resume systems are set up to read skills. Place the important skills at the beginning of the resume where employers can see them first. Also, scannable database systems store a fixed number of skills so that those that come later may not be included in the database. Insure that your skills and occupation-specific keywords match your objective.

- Place your name, address, and phone number with area code in a block format below the top margin. This key information helps interested employers reach you and is the preferred format for scannable systems. Put your name on each page.

- Use generous margins and plenty of white space. One-inch margins enhance the readability of your resume. Balance the body of the resume so the content is not compressed. For multiple pages, make sure information is balanced on the pages. The final resume should be a high-contrast image— dark ink on white or light-colored paper.

- Use vertical and horizontal lines sparingly and include a quarter-inch of space around them. (Scanning systems can confuse lines and characters.)

- Avoid graphics and shading. Shading reduces the contrast, making text hard to read. Graphics may catch the human eye but do not make sense to scanning systems.

- Use a font size between 10 and 14 points. Don't use *script*, *italic*, or underlining. Highlight information using **bold** or CAPITAL letters.

- Stapling or folding diminishes the visual appearance of the resume and affects scannability. Avoid fasteners and consider sending your resume flat in a large white envelope.

- Be sure your resume is high quality and professional. Laser print your final copy. Remember, this is your advertisement to employers.

- Choose a typeface (font) that is easily readable rather than decorative. Times, AGaramond, Optima, Caslon Book, or Slimbach are readable.

Resumes and Cover Letters

General Resume Guidelines

DO'S	DON'TS
• Lead with your strongest statements that are related to the job or goal.	• Do not use abbreviations (exceptions include middle initial and directions such as N for North).
• Emphasize your skills.	• Do not use "I" to refer to yourself.
• Keep it brief (1-2 pages).	• Avoid any mention of salary expectations or wage history.
• Use 8 1/2" x 11" paper.	
• Correct all typographical, grammatical, and spelling errors.	• Do not print on a dot matrix printer.
• Include your employment-related accomplishments.	• Do not use fancy typeset, binders, or exotic paper.
• Target your qualifications.	• Do not send a photograph of yourself.
• Clearly communicate your purpose and value to employers.	• Do not make statements that you cannot prove.
• Maintain eye-appealing visual appearance.	• Do not include personal information (age, height, weight, family status, picture, or religious or political affiliation unless you are applying for a job with one of these organizations).
• Use the best format to showcase your skills.	
• Appear neat, well organized, and professional.	• Do not change the tense of verbs or use the passive voice.
• Be creative and make your resume relevant to the job.	• It is not necessary to use the title "resume."
• Always include a cover letter when mailing your resume.	• Do not include references on the resume. Make a separate reference sheet.
• To enhance your qualifications, use measurable outcomes, values, and percentages.	• Do not include hobbies or social interests unless they contribute to your objective.
	• Do not staple or fold your resume.

CREATIVE Job Search

Resumes and Cover Letters

Resume Preparation

Quality Paper

Now that you have invested time in writing the perfect resume, what remains is to produce a high-quality final product. Quality paper is a final touch that will leave a favorable impression with a prospective employer. It is appealing to the eye and prints better, maintaining a clear, sharp image. As for color, white is still considered the first choice. Off-white, cream, or gray is acceptable; avoid using colored paper. Paper size should be the standard letter size, 8-1/2" x 11."

Paper Weight

Quality paper should be between 16 and 25 lbs. One hundred percent cotton fiber (rag content) is the best.

Production

When creating your original or master, it should be produced using a common word processing or desktop publishing program. Typing your resume on a standard typewriter should be avoided since its print is usually not high quality. Editing and modifying will also be difficult. If all you have is a standard typewriter, consider taking your final draft to someone for word processing.

Paper Texture

Personal preference should be your guide. Examples include: linen, pebble finish, and vellum. Avoid glossy or high shine finishes.

Reproduction

When making copies for distribution, laser printing is preferred. Due to the poor quality, never print your resume on a dot matrix printer. You may also choose to have a print shop print your resume. If you reproduce your resume on a photocopier, be sure that the copies are clear, clean, and sharp.

Computer Resources

Computers have become an important job search tool for most job seekers. There are many places where use of a computer costs very little or is free. For example:

- Minnesota WorkForce Centers
- Friends and Family
- Schools
- Social organizations
- Community agencies
- Print shops
- Religious organizations
- Private placement agencies
- Libraries

Resumes and Cover Letters

SAMPLES AND WORKSHEETS

The following resume samples model the basic formats and principles of resume writing. Consider how each job seeker presented his/her skills and experience. Along with the content, look at how the resume is presented. Draw the best from each to help decide how to style your resume. Ultimately, your resume will be unique to you and will not look exactly like any of these presented. For more resume samples, look in the job search section of your local book store or library, or contact your local Job Service office.

Your resume should focus on your skills. Employers want to know what you can do, not just where you have been. That is why resume scanning systems look for skills. The second copy of each resume has keywords highlighted that a resume scanning system might identify. Various scanning systems will identify different skills. This is because resume scanning systems use a lexicon or dictionary when looking for words and will identify only those words that are on file.

The resume worksheets are tools for crafting your resume. They are not intended as a fill-in-the-blank form. Use them as models. Sections may vary and the layout you choose will ultimately be a variation on one or all of these formats.

> "Your resume is a marketing tool.
>
> Make sure it presents you in a positive way."

Resumes and Cover Letters

Chronological Resume Sample: Work-to-Work Job Seeker

ELIZABETH B. JOBSEEKER
5555 Lakewood Road
Somewhere, Minnesota 55555
(555) 555-5555

OBJECTIVE: Mechanical Engineer

ENGINEERING EXPERIENCE:

Industrial Engineer — 199_ - 200_
Tool Incorporated Minnetonka, MN
- Designed a plant layout for the shipping department
- Developed a multi-step shipping process improvement plan

Design Engineer — 199_ - 199_
Mechanical Systems St. Paul, MN
- Developed a complete safety package for a robot loader
- Designed hydraulic double stack lift
- Redesigned dairy open style conveyor
- Trained 10 engineers on Autocad Rev. 12
- Evaluated and purchased machine components

HVAC Engineer Assistant — 199_ - 199_
Engineering Consultants St. Paul, MN
- Prepared building and equipment bid specifications
- Evaluated HVAC equipment options
- Incorporated EPA and OSHA regulations into safety procedures
- Created working drawing on Autocad Rev. 1

MANAGEMENT EXPERIENCE:

Supervisor — 198_ - 198_
College Police Department Minneapolis, MN
- Supervised over 50 student security personnel
- Maintained security accounts and budgets
- Interviewed, hired, field trained, and conducted performance appraisals
- Prepared 25-page monthly report

Manager — 198_ - 198_
Building Management Co. Northwoods, MN
- Maintained and performed building improvements

EDUCATION:

Bachelor of Science Degree: **Mechanical Engineering** 199_
Minor: Engineering Management
University of Minnesota, Minneapolis, MN

Course Work: Thermodynamics, Heat Transfer, HVAC, Machine Design, Fluid Power, IBM Compatible, Autocad 12, FORTRAN, Lotus, and Quattro Pro

Chronological Resume Sample: School-to-Work Job Seeker

DEBRA JOBSEEKER, L. P. N.
5555 Lakewood Road
Somewhere, Minnesota 55555
(555) 555-5555

SUMMARY:

Highly-motivated, dependable **Licensed Practical Nurse**. Proven ability to initiate appropriate action, follow instructions, and carry out tasks in an efficient manner. Proficient in patient care, medical management, coordination, and emergency room technique. Team player with effective interpersonal communication skills, and a positive, can-do attitude.

EDUCATION:

Certificate: Licensed Practical Nurse Program (GPA: 3.85/4.0)   2000
Normandale Community College, Bloomtown, MN

Internship: Regions Hospital   St. Paul, MN   3 Months   2000
- Infection Control   • Critical Care   • Injections
- Catheter Care   • Vital Signs   • Triage
- Blood Draw   • Charting   • Intake
- IV Therapy   • CPR   • Acute Care

Diploma: Richfield Senior High School   Richfield, MN   199_

RELATED VOLUNTEER EXPERIENCE:

American Red Cross Minneapolis, MN   199_ - 199_
- Provided emergency services to people in crisis.
- Assisted in providing information and services regarding food, shelter, clothing, and medical provisions.

Courage Center Golden Valley, MN   199_ - 199_
- Assisted disabled patients with daily living activities by writing letters, reading correspondence, feeding, pushing wheelchairs, and shopping.

Neighborhood Involvement Program St. Paul, MN   199_ - 199_
- Organized a block safety program for 26 households which reduced crime in the area by 15 percent.

MEMBERSHIPS:

Elected Secretary: Parent Teachers Association   199_

Functional Resume Sample: Work-to-Work Job Seeker

JERRY J. JOB
5555 Lakewood Road
Somewhere, Minnesota 55555
(555) 555-5555

OBJECTIVE
Dependable, enthusiastic worker with over 10 years of experience seeking a Welding or Building Maintenance position. Self-starter, dedicated to achieving high-quality results.

SUMMARY OF QUALIFICATIONS

Welding—
Developed extensive experience in a wide variety of welding styles and positions including:

- MIG
- TIG
- ARC
- Heliarc
- Oxyacetylene
- Air ARC
- Cutting & Gouging
- Automatic Seam
- Plasma Cutting
- Underwater
- Water Cooled Spot Welding

Fabrication—
Skilled in layout and design of sheet metal and pipe. Developed extensive knowledge of sheet rollers and brakes. Followed Manufacturer's Operating Processes (MOP) to detail.

Equipment Operator—
Experienced forklift operator on various sizes and styles of forklifts. Skilled in the use of a variety of power tools and metal fabrication equipment including: drills, drill press, edge planer, end mill, benders, power saws, sanders, and grinders.

Equipment Maintenance—
Performed general maintenance on welding equipment and production machinery. Maintained high production levels through on site machine repairs and preventive maintenance.

Building Maintenance—
Acquired experience in general construction including basic electrical repairs, carpentry, concrete, glass, spray and roller painting, plumbing, patching, and sheetrock.

SUMMARY OF EXPERIENCE

Lead Welder
- Maintained strict performance, quality, and production standards.
- Trained new employees and monitored performance during probation.

EDUCATION
Certificate: Welding and Blueprint Reading
Somewhere Technical College - Somewhere, MN
Diploma: Somewhere Senior High School - Somewhere, MN

Functional Resume Sample: No Paid Work Experience

JOE DOER
5555 Lakewood Road
Somewhere, Minnesota 55555
(555) 555-5555

EMPLOYMENT OBJECTIVE
Assembly, Janitorial, Maintenance, or Construction Work

SUMMARY OF SKILLS
- Industrious, reliable, highly-motivated and thorough
- Ability to safely operate power machines, tools, saws, sanders, and drills
- Operate, repair and maintain mowers, snow blowers, buffers, and trucks
- Experience with household repairs, painting, siding, and construction

RELATED VOLUNTEER EXPERIENCE
Assembly
- Received, sorted, bundled, and placed recycling articles in correct containers
- Assembled, cleaned, and packaged toys for children on holidays
- Repaired bicycles, motor bikes, and garage doors
- Assisted nursing home residents with making crafts and decorating rooms

Janitorial
- Maintained all aspects of home, and made minor repairs to structures and equipment
- Assisted neighbors and friends with lawn care, mowing, raking, shoveling, painting, buffing, sanding, remodeling, and cleaning.
- Helped residents repair and clean homes after a flood

Construction
- Assisted in building or remodeling homes for low-income families
- Sanded floors, walls, and cupboards
- Laid sheet rock, painted and stained woodwork, mixed cement, and sided outside walls
- Constructed emergency Mash Units and troop quarters. Drove and repaired trucks.

VOLUNTEER WORK HISTORY
Goodwill Industries	St. Paul, MN
Minnesota Flood Victims Rescue	East Grand Forks, MN
Habitat for Humanity	St. Paul, MN
Sunshine Nursing Home	Minneapolis, MN

EDUCATION
Diploma: Johnson High School - St. Paul, MN
Honorable Discharge: United States Army - Private E3 Classification

Combination Resume Sample: No Paid Work Experience

SHIRLEY I. QUALIFY
5555 Transferability Road
Somewhere, MN 55555
(555) 555-5555

SUMMARY
Dependable **General Office Worker** with over 10 years of transferable experience. Proven clerical, customer service, and communication skills in a variety of settings. Upbeat, positive attitude with a history of producing quality results and satisfied customers. Computer literate.

SELECTED SKILLS

General Office
- Organized and implemented group activities in an efficient manner
- Scheduled appointments and assured timely arrival
- Maintained accurate financial records, and paid all invoices on time
- Answered phones and took accurate messages
- Prepared reports and created documents using MS Word and WordPerfect
- Located desired information using the Internet

Customer Service
- Welcomed customers and visitors in a friendly and courteous manner
- Provided customers/clients with desired information in a timely manner
- Listened, calmed, and assisted customers with concerns
- Established friendly and lasting relationships

Communication
- Utilized Internet E-Mail as an effective communication tool
- Answered phones in a courteous and professional manner
- Established rapport with diverse individuals and groups
- Demonstrated ability to express ideas in a team environment and influence action

RELATED VOLUNTEER EXPERIENCE

General Office Volunteer	Salvation Army St. Paul, MN	5 Years
Elected Secretary	Parent Teachers Association (ISD 11) Anoka, MN	5 Years
Event Coordinator	Neighborhood Involvement Program St. Paul, MN	3 Years
Group/Activities Leader	Girl Scouts of America St. Paul, MN	4 Years
Family Manager	Self-Employed Anoka, MN	7 Years

EDUCATION
GED: Ramsey Action Program St. Paul, MN

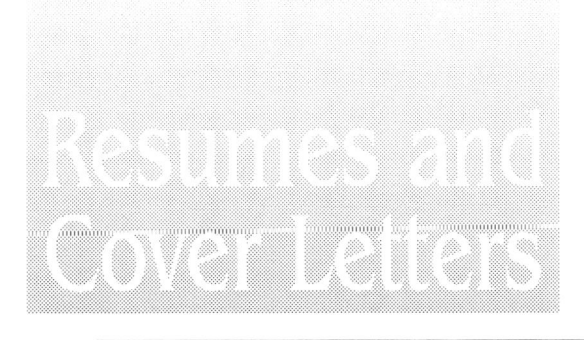

Combination Resume Sample: Work-to-Work Job Seeker

RED E. JOBHUNTER
5555 Lakewood Road
Somewhere, Minnesota 55555
(555) 555-5555

Medical Laboratory Technician

Extensive experience as a registered Medical Laboratory Technician with proven competencies in Phlebotomy, Instrument Maintenance, Teaching, and Quality Control in a laboratory setting.

SUMMARY OF SKILLS & EXPERIENCE

Laboratory
- Regarded as a highly-skilled lab technologist, with experience serving ER, Urgent Care, Pediatric ER, and Stab-Room Trauma Unit.
- Processed cultures in microbiology, gram stains, urinalysis, and various manual tests.
- Increased lab efficiency through improved procedures, research and development of technical equipment, and lab layout and design.

Phlebotomy
- Performed both inpatient and outpatient, pre-op and post-op, blood draws.
- Recognized for exceptional skill in serving hard to draw patients and children.

Instrument Maintenance
- Skilled in troubleshooting and maintenance of technical equipment.
- Maintained on line performance and peak output.

Teaching
- Mastered teaching techniques.
- Recognized for excellent communication skills.
- Trained staff effectively on complex equipment operation and procedures.

Quality Control
- Maintained high quality standards with an emphasis on accuracy within strict guidelines.
- Maximized lab performance through organization, equipment testing, and procedure development.

EMPLOYMENT HISTORY

Medical Laboratory Technician, ASCP   199_ - 199_
   Hennepin County Medical Center   Minneapolis, MN
Phlebotomist   199_ - 199_
   Minneapolis Children's Medical Center   Minneapolis, MN

EDUCATION

Certificate: Medical Laboratory Technician (GPA 3.5/4.0)
   College of St. Catherine - St. Paul, MN
Certificate: American Society of Clinical Pathologists
Course Work: Biology/Chemistry (117 credits)
   Minnesota State University - Mankato, MN

Resumes and Cover Letters

Chronological Resume Worksheet

This is a general format. Actual content and layout will vary. Not all items are required or necessary.

Name _____
Address _____
Phone (____) _____ Fax (____) _____
E-Mail _____

EMPLOYMENT OBJECTIVE (Optional) _____

SUMMARY (Optional—can include on cover letter) _____
_____
_____

WORK EXPERIENCE

Company, City, State _____
Job Title _____ Dates _____
Responsibilities/Accomplishments/Skills _____
_____
_____
_____

Company, City, State _____
Job Title _____ Dates _____
Responsibilities/Accomplishments/Skills _____
_____
_____
_____

Company, City, State _____
Job Title _____ Dates _____
Responsibilities/Accomplishments/Skills _____
_____
_____
_____

EDUCATION _____

LICENSES AND CERTIFICATIONS _____

AWARDS _____

PROFESSIONAL MEMBERSHIPS _____

CREATIVE Job Search

Resumes and Cover Letters

Functional Resume Worksheet

This is a general format. Actual content and layout will vary. Not all items are required or necessary.

Name _____

Address _____

Phone (___) _____ Fax (___) _____

E-Mail _____

EMPLOYMENT OBJECTIVE (Optional)
_____
_____

HIGHLIGHTS OF QUALIFICATIONS (Optional)
_____
_____

WORK EXPERIENCE

Occupational/Functional Category _____
Skills/Accomplishments/Responsibilities _____
_____
_____
_____

Occupational/Functional Category _____
Skills/Accomplishments/Responsibilities _____
_____
_____
_____

Occupational/Functional Category _____
Skills/Accomplishments/Responsibilities _____
_____
_____
_____

EMPLOYMENT HISTORY

Company _____ Title _____ Dates _____
Company _____ Title _____ Dates _____
Company _____ Title _____ Dates _____

EDUCATION
LICENSES AND CERTIFICATION
AWARDS/PROFESSIONAL MEMBERSHIPS

CREATIVE Job Search

Resumes and Cover Letters

Combination Resume Worksheet

This is a general format. Actual content and layout will vary. Not all items are required or necessary.

Name _____
Address _____
Phone (___) _____ Fax (___) _____
E-Mail _____

Employment Objective _____

Summary of Skills and/or Experience
Skill/Experience _____
Description _____

Skill/Experience _____
Description _____

Skill/Experience _____
Description _____

Employment History
Name of
Company _____ Job Title _____

Address/Phone _____ Dates of Employment _____

Name of
Company _____ Job Title _____

Address/Phone _____ Dates of Employment _____

Name of
Company _____ Job Title _____

Address/Phone _____ Dates of Employment _____

Education
School Name _____

City/State _____ Dates of Attendance (if recent) _____

Major(s) _____

Degree/Certificate Earned _____

Licenses and Certifications _____

Professional Memberships/Organizations _____

CREATIVE Job Search 72

Resumes and Cover Letters

RESUME STRATEGIES

How to Use Your Resume Effectively

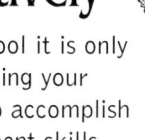

A good resume is an important job search tool, but like any tool it is only as good as the person using it. Much has been said about selling your employment skills to a prospective employer. What it takes to accomplish this is job search skills. It is not enough to have the employment skills that an employer desires if you do not have the ability to market them. Use your resume effectively when networking.

Now that you have perfected your resume, there are some guidelines for using it effectively. Job search strategies range from the simple and common to the innovative and complex. Following are some of the more common strategies and guidelines. The successful job seeker will master these skills.

Give your resume to:

- Minnesota WorkForce Centers
- Employers with advertised job openings
- Employers with no advertised job openings
- Private and public employment agencies
- Vocational and college placement offices
- Personal and professional networking contacts
- Your references
- Executive recruiters
- Your instructors

Resumes and Cover Letters

Tips For Using Your Resume

- Resumes should be sent to a person by name. Avoid sending the resume to a job title such as "Production Manager." It will take extra effort, but do your research and find out the name and title of the appropriate person to whom your resume should be sent.

- If you are asked to send your resume to personnel or human resources, do so. Then also send a resume to the person in charge of the department in which you want to work. Most of the time, personnel does the screening; it is the department manager who is the final hiring authority.

- When mailing your resume, always send it with a cover letter. Never send it by itself.

- Mass-mailing your resume to many employers, hoping that a couple of them will get someone's attention, is not effective. The statistics are that for every 1,000 resumes you send to an employer, you can expect to get two interviews. Additionally, an accepted standard is that for every ten interviews, you will receive one job offer.

- Look for ways to target your resume to the specific needs of the employer. This can be accomplished with a targeted resume or through the cover letter. It requires some research before sending the resume, but it will pay off in an increased number of positive responses.

- When researching an employer or employment agency, among other important information, find out if they use a resume scanning system. If they do, it will help you prepare your resume for presentation.

- Send your resume to employers even if they are not hiring. You never know what the future will bring.

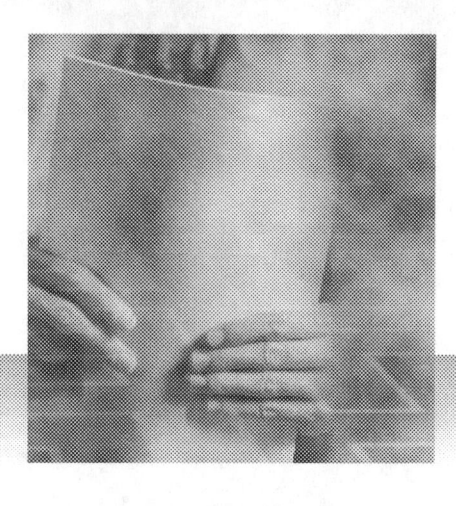

- Always follow-up the sending of your resume with a phone call to the employer. Be courteous, professional, and sell your qualifications. Be sure to ask for an interview.

- When directly contacting employers, always have a copy of your resume available and take the initiative to offer it to them.

- When applying for a job with an employment application, you may want to attach your resume. The resume will add impact and should complement the application. If you are asked to fill out an application, never write on it "See resume." Take the time to fill out the application completely.

- Applying for jobs by resume can be effective in overcoming employment barriers. The resume should paint the best picture of you, while the application may paint the worst.

- Give a copy of your resume to your references. It provides them with information about you and will help them to talk to an employer about your qualifications.

- Give a copy of your resume to all networking contacts. It is an excellent ice breaker to use the resume as a center for discussing your qualifications. Ask your contacts to critique your resume.

- Always bring extra copies of your resume to an interview.

- Finally, **Follow-up, Follow-up, Follow-up!**

- It is no use mailing resumes if you do not take the time to follow up on your efforts. If you are not getting responses or interviews from your resume, you may want to reevaluate it. The true test of an effective resume is that you are offered interviews.

Resumes and Cover Letters

Resume Critique Form

Use this form to rate your resume, or have someone familiar with your career field rate it. Grade the resume in each category as EXCELLENT, AVERAGE, or POOR. Write in suggestions for improvement.

Item	Excellent	Average	Poor	*Unknown	Improvements
1. Appearance Does it look good without reading it?					
2. Format Was the best format used to sell your strengths?					
3. Skills Is the resume skill-based? Count the skills _____					
4. Keywords Are keywords and phrases easy to identify?					
5. Focus Does the content point to your employment objective?					
6. Scannability Is it designed to be easily read by a scanning system?					
7. Proofing Is it free from grammar, spelling, or typing errors?					
8. Length Is it a reasonable length?					
9. Integrity Is it an honest presentation of your best qualities?					
10. Appropriate Does the content capture an employer's interest?					

* If you are unsure, then review these topics before finishing your resume.

Resumes and Cover Letters

COVER LETTERS

The resume is a description of your qualifications, much like a product brochure. When presenting the resume to an employer, it needs to be personalized and targeted. The cover letter is your opportunity to personalize your resume and target your skills.

Most letter formats can be used for the cover letter. The only absolute is that it conform to accepted standards for business letters. The reader of a cover letter may be the hiring authority, an agent of the hiring authority, or an interested third party. The hiring authority is the person who has the final say in who is hired for a specific position (ultimately, this is the person you want to read your resume). An agent is usually someone who is working on behalf of the hiring authority, such as: personnel or human resources, an independent agency or a subordinate. Third parties include colleagues and subordinates of the hiring authority who are assisting in the hiring, as well as networking or referral contacts. The way you craft your letter should take the reader into consideration. A cover letter may be sent in response to an advertised job opening, or a referral from a networking contact, or directly to an employer.

Any time a resume is sent by mail, it must be accompanied by a cover letter.

Resumes and Cover Letters

Cover Letter Formats

Invited Letter — This letter format is used when an employer has solicited the resume for consideration. This is often in response to a want-ad or publicized job listing. This style focuses on matching your qualifications to the advertised requirements of the position.

Uninvited or Cold-Contact Letter — Use this format to contact employers who have not advertised or published job openings. The focus is on matching your qualifications to the perceived needs of the employer based on labor market research. This strategy requires that a phone or personal contact with the employer either precede or follow the sending of the resume and cover letter.

Referral Letter — Through networking, informational interviews, and contact with employers, the effective job seeker will receive referrals to job opportunities. These referrals may be to a specific job opening (advertised or unadvertised), or to an employer who may or may not be hiring now. In a referral letter, mention the individual who provided the information about the company or job.

Cover Letter Variation

Job Match or "T" Letter — When crafting a cover letter, it is always important to match your qualifications to the job and/or employer. Some sources for information include employment advertisements, position descriptions, phone conversations, and informational interviews. Generally, this is done in the narrative of the letter. The "T" letter format uses bulleted comparisons that target the specific requirements and your corresponding qualifications.

Cover Letter Points to Consider

- State the date and your name and address at the top of the letter.

- Below your name and address, write the name and address of the person to whom you are writing. Always address the letter to a specific person by name and title. Even if responding to a job that states "no phone calls," consider calling to politely ask the name of the hiring authority. You may not always be able to identify the name of a specific person. In this case, send the letter to the title of the recipient (Production Manager, Maintenance Supervisor, Office Manager, Human Resources, or Search Committee). Do not use "To Whom It May Concern."

- State your interest in the job for which you are applying.

- Mention your skills, education, special training, and work experience that qualify you for the job.

- Provide a phone number and a time you will be available so the employer can reach you.

- Thank the person for taking the time to read your letter.

- Use the appropriate closing, such as "Sincerely."

- Ask someone to proofread your letter to check content, grammar, and spelling.

- State a time when you will call the employer to follow-up.

- Sign the letter in blue ink. It implies the letter is original and may get more attention. The only other ink color to use is black. Never use any other color on the cover letter.

- Structure the letter to reflect your individuality, but avoid appearing too familiar, overbearing, humorous, or cute. Keep sentences short and to the point.

- Keep it brief, usually no more than one page with three to five paragraphs.

- Use the same paper stock for both your cover letter and resume.

Resumes and Cover Letters

Job Match or "T" Sample

Your Name
Address
City, State Zip Code
Phone Number

February 25, 200_

Ms. Jane Smith, Title
Work Incorporated
555 Pine Street
St. Paul, MN 55555

Dear Ms. Smith:

I am very interested in the position of Administrative Assistant listed in the Daily Tribune on February 24, 2001. The skills and qualifications you mention closely match my experience in this career field.

Your Needs:	My Qualifications:
• Detail-oriented, experienced Administrative Assistant	• Four years Administrative Assistant experience with responsibility for numerous detailed reports
• Assist Customer Relations Manager	• Assisted Customer Relations Manager for two years
• Corporate experience with major clients a must	• Regularly served purchasing agents at Fortune 500 companies
• PC knowledge a plus	• Hands-on experience with Lotus 1-2-3 and WordPerfect on IBM-PC

Enclosed is my resume for your review and consideration. I believe I am an excellent candidate for this position, and look forward to meeting with you to discuss it in greater detail. I will plan to call you on (*date*) to determine when an interview might be possible. Thank you.

Sincerely,

(*Signature*)
Typed Name

Enclosure

Resumes and Cover Letters

Cover Letter Samples

Your Name
Street Address
City, State Zip Code
Phone Number

Date

Individual's Name
Job Title
Name of Organization
Street Address
City, State Zip Code

Dear Mr./Ms. _____:

First Paragraph: State the reason for writing. Name the specific position or type of work for which you are applying. Mention how you learned of the opening.

Second Paragraph: Explain why you are interested in working for this employer and specify how you are PERFECT for this position. Do not only repeat the information on your resume. Include something special or unique about yourself that would "benefit" the employer. Remember, the reader will consider this an example of your writing skills.

Third Paragraph: Mention your resume is enclosed and indicate your desire to meet with the employer. You may want to suggest alternate dates and times, or simply advise them of your flexibility to the time and place. Include day and evening contact information. Include a statement or question that will encourage the reader to respond. Be sure to communicate your plan to follow up. You might state that you will be in the area on a certain date and would like to set up a meeting, or you will call on a certain date to set up a meeting. Never leave it up to the employer to get in touch with you. Finally, thank the employer for his/her time.

Sincerely,

(Your Signature in blue or black ink)
Your typed name

Enclosure

Cold-Contact Cover Letter Sample

Karen Kareer
5555 Lakewood Road
Somewhere, MN 55555
(555) 555-5555

May 20, 200_

Ms. Francisca Favor
Department Manager
EFTG Industries, Inc.
210 Industry Avenue
Anytown, MN 55555

Dear Ms. Favor:

Perhaps you are seeking an addition to your marketing team. A new person can provide innovative approaches to the challenges of marketing. I am an innovator of new ideas, an excellent communicator with buyers, and have a demonstrated history of marketing success.

Presently, I am marketing computer products for a major supplier using television, radio, and news advertising. I have a reputation for putting forth the effort required to make a project succeed.

Enclosed is my resume for your review and consideration. EFTG Industries has a reputation for excellence. I would like to use my talents to market your quality line of technical products. I will call you on May 28, 200_ to further discuss my talents and how I can benefit your company. If you prefer, you may reach me in the evenings at (555) 555-5555.

Thank you for your time. I look forward to meeting with you.

Sincerely,

Karen Kareer

Enclosure

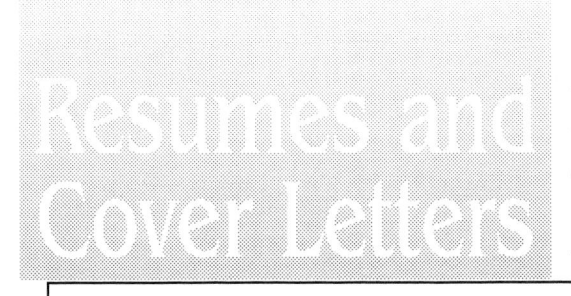

Invited Cover Letter Sample

Johnny Network
5555 Lakewood Road
Somewhere, MN 55555
(555) 555-5555

June 26, 200_

Mr. Phillip Morework
Production Manager
XYZ Corporation
21 Industry Lane
Anytown, MN 55555

Dear Mr. Morework:

Please consider my qualifications for the **Lead Production Assistant** opportunity, which was listed in the Daily Planet on *date*. With a proven high-tech background in Fortune 100 companies, I am well qualified and eager to represent your company in this capacity.

I thrive in a fast-paced environment where production deadlines are a priority, and handling multiple jobs simultaneously is the norm. In relation to leadership, I have been responsible for up to 35 staff members, and have built a reputation for making quality administrative decisions in a fair and consistent manner. Constant negotiations with all levels of management and staff have strengthened my interpersonal skills.

I am looking forward to discussing my qualifications with you. Enclosed is my resume for your review and consideration. I will call you on *date* to confirm receipt of this information, and discuss possible next steps. Thank you very much for your time and consideration.

Sincerely,

Johnny Network

Enclosure

Resumes and Cover Letters

Invited Cover Letter Sample — No Paid Work Experience

Wanda Job

5555 Lakewood Road
Somewhere, MN 55555
(555) 555-5555

January 6, 200_

Ms. Marilyn Payer
Housekeeping Manager
Rodetown Inn
123 Indiana Drive
Anytown, MN 55555

Dear Ms. Payer:

Your ad for a **Housekeeper** in the Jobs Now newspaper on Sunday, January 4, 200_ caught my eye. I have several years of housekeeping and home maintenance experience, and believe that I have the necessary skills for the position. My resume is enclosed for your consideration.

Rodetown Inn has an excellent reputation in the community as a quality employer, and my skills perfectly match the requirements. Having been a homeowner for over five years, I do all of my own maintenance and repair. I also have four years of experience as a home care volunteer for the Salvation Army's "Be Friends" program. This includes helping disabled, elderly persons with household chores such as: bed making, cleaning, vacuuming, dusting, laundry, washing walls, windows, mopping, mowing, raking, and shoveling. I am known to be extremely reliable, efficient, organized, and a good team worker.

It would be beneficial for us to meet to discuss the position and my qualifications in greater detail. I will contact you on _date_ to determine when a convenient interview time might be arranged. Please feel free to contact me in the interim at the number shown above. Thank you for your time. I look forward to talking with you soon.

Sincerely,

Wanda Job

Enclosure

Resumes and Cover Letters

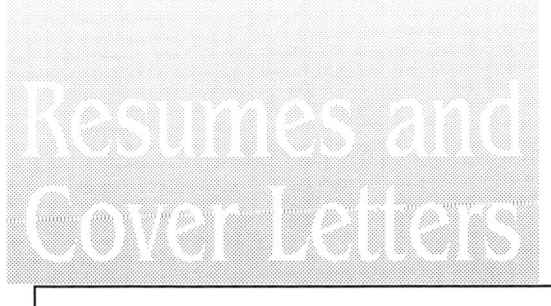

Referral Cover Letter Sample

Susan Jones

5555 Lakewood Road
Somewhere, MN 55555
(555) 555-5555

July 31, 200_

Ms. Rhonda Leland
Corporate Manager
Do-It Corporation
42 Industry Circle
Somewhere Else, MN 55555

Dear Ms. Leland:

Mary Smith, Vice President of Marketing with Do-It Corporation, suggested that I contact you directly regarding my interest in an **Administrative Assistant** position with your organization. Although my resume is actively on file in Human Resources, Ms. Smith felt that you would want to be made aware of my unique qualifications and availability. Consequently, I have enclosed my resume for your consideration.

I am a highly qualified Administrative Assistant with more than four years of experience serving executive management for a large manufacturing company. My qualifications include extensive PC experience with the software used at Do-It Corp. (Powerpoint, Excel, & MS Office 2001), proven customer service skills, itinerary planning, and report writing.

I will be in your area on August 20, 200_ (9:00 - 3:00), and would appreciate an opportunity to meet with you to discuss my qualifications in greater detail. I will plan to contact you on *date*, to arrange a possible meeting time.

Thank you for your time and consideration.

Sincerely,

Susan Jones

Enclosure

cc: M. Smith

Resumes and Cover Letters

NOTES

Job Search Tools

5

The right tools make any job easier.

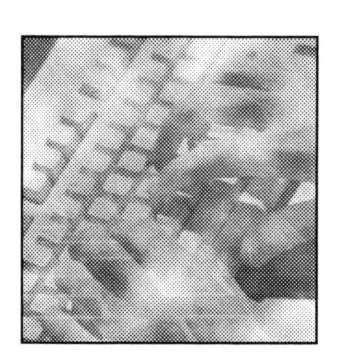

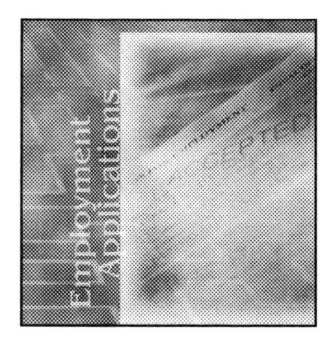

Choose your references with care.

Employment Applications

Job Search Tools

Many occupations require specific tools. A successful job search also requires specific "tools." This chapter covers many of these job search tools and their uses.

Information will be presented on:

- Employment Applications
- Completing an Application
- Letters of Recommendation
- Performance Evaluations
- Personal Data Sheet
- References
- Work Samples

EMPLOYMENT APPLICATIONS

Employment applications are an important part of your job search. Some employers require the application as the first step in the selection process. Others may not require it until later. No matter when the application is requested, it is an important job search tool. It provides an opportunity to sell your qualifications. The completed application may be the first impression the employer has of you.

The employment application is used to obtain information about your qualifications and to compare you to other applicants. Companies may receive hundreds or even thousands of applications each year. Therefore, they look for ways to reduce the number of applications they will read thoroughly. The employer "screens out" many applicants based on various factors in the application. You need to do everything possible to create the "perfect" application. Following are some general guidelines for completing applications.

Visual Impact

It is a good idea to make a copy of the application in case you make a mistake. Fill out the application completely, neatly, and with no errors in grammar or spelling. Print clearly in black ink, do not use abbreviations, and respond to all questions. Use N/A (not applicable) if the section does not apply to you. This shows the employer that you made an honest effort to fill out the entire application; you didn't overlook anything. If you are seeking professional or office jobs, you may want to type the application.

Follow Directions

Read the entire application before you complete it. Pay close attention to what is being asked and how you are expected to respond. Read and respect sections that say, "Do Not Write Below This Line," or "Office Use Only." These sections may give insight into the evaluation process.

Be Positive

During your job search you want to present a positive, honest picture of yourself. Avoid any negative information. Look for ways that show you are the right person for the job. Think of what you would look for in an employee if you were an employer.

Be Honest

You must be truthful on an application. The information you provide may become part of your permanent employment record. False information can become the basis for dismissal. Provide only the information the employer is seeking or is necessary to sell your qualifications.

Job Search Tools

Target Your Qualifications

Many applications have limited space to display your skills, experience, and accomplishments. Increase your chances of gaining an interview by carefully selecting what you will include on the application. Display your qualifications that meet the specific needs of the job. Read the job description carefully. Advance knowledge of the company, its products or services, and especially the skills needed to do the job will help you choose the appropriate information to include. For ideas and techniques on doing employer research, read Discover Where the Jobs Are on page 28.

Position Desired

Employers will not try to figure out where you fit in their organization. If the job is an advertised job or if you are looking for a specific position, enter that job title in the blank space provided. When you are not applying for a specific position, state the name of the department in which you wish to work. If you are interested in more than one job, fill out more than one application.

Job Gaps

If you have job gaps in your employment history, be sure to think of positive ways you were spending your time while unemployed. Make your answer short, simple, and truthful. Examples include managing and maintaining a household, attending school, and providing child care. If you were volunteering for an organization, be sure to state the name of the organization and the type of work you were doing. This will prepare you to answer questions regarding your job gap.

Salary Requirements

When asked about salary requirements, it is best to give a salary range or to respond with "negotiable." Use one of these responses even if you know the wage. You never know what the future holds, and you could negotiate a higher salary. Remember that questions about salary may be "knockout" questions used to reduce the number of applicants.

REASONS FOR LEAVING

Carefully choose your words when responding to this question. Negative responses may provide a swift way for the employer to eliminate your application from consideration. When stating why you left a job, it is important to avoid using the words "fired," "quit," "illness," or "personal reasons." These responses may reduce your chances of being hired. Always look for positive statements. If you respond with, "Will explain at the interview," you can expect to be called on to do so. Often there are better ways to respond. Think of a way you can put your reason in a positive light. Examples: "Returned to school to learn new skills," or "To find a job that more closely matched my skills."

Fired

Do not use the term "fired" or "terminated." Find a phrase that sounds neutral such as "involuntary separation." You may want to call past employers to find out what they will say in response to reference checks. When contacting former employers, reintroduce yourself and explain that you are looking for a new job. Ask what they will say if they are contacted for a reference check. If you were terminated, you may want to request that this employer simply verify your dates of employment, job title, and describe your job duties. You may also consider having a confidante call and ask for a reference, then report to you what is said. In the future, if you are faced with being terminated, you may request that the employer's record documents a mutually agreeable reason for separation, and explain you are concerned that a record saying you were "terminated" may have a negative impact on your employability.

Quit for a better job. This response includes: leaving for advancement potential, leaving to work closer to home, leaving for a better work environment, or leaving for a career change. If you quit for a better job, there should not be a long break in employment; your employment history should support the statement.

Quit to move to another area. In this case, you quit without having another job. You may have moved to be nearer to your family, to an area with greater economic potential, to an area better suited for raising children, etc. Be careful not to use this reason for more than one employer on your application as it might appear you are not a dependable or stable employee.

Quit to attend school. If you use this reason, the education listed on your application and/or resume must agree. Preferably, your school program is consistent with your career goals. You should assure the employer any continuing school activities will not interfere with the job.

Quit

If you quit your job, be prepared to offer an explanation. If you quit under less than favorable conditions, avoid saying anything negative about the employer. You may want to use the term "resigned" or "voluntarily separated" which implies you followed proper procedures in leaving the job. There are many positive, valid reasons why you may have quit your job. You should be prepared to explain the reason on the application and/or in the interview.

Other reasons for quitting a job include volunteer work (state what kind of work and with whom you did volunteer work), starting your own business, or raising your family. In all of these cases, you need to assure the employer you are now fully ready to assume the responsibilities of the job.

Laid off

If you were laid off from a job due to no fault of your own, tell the employer the circumstances. Phrases you might want to use include lack of work, lack of operating funds, temporary employment, seasonal employment, company closed, plant closing, company downsized, a corporate merger, etc.

Job Search Tools

COMPLETING AN APPLICATION

Just as a tool box contains many tools to get a job done, the following are some more ideas to help you "get the job" done.

Illegal Questions

Applications may contain questions that are tricky or even illegal. These may include questions about age, gender, disabilities, health, marital status, children, race, arrests or convictions, religion, and workers' compensation. Read the application first so you can plan your answer. You need to decide how you will respond. If the question does not bother you, answer it. If it does bother you, you may want to use N/A or a dash (—). Keep in mind you may get screened out by having too many of these responses. Additional information about illegal questions can be found at a Minnesota WorkForce Center, the Attorney General's office, or the Human Rights office.

Letters of Recommendation

Letters of recommendation are written evaluations of your work performance and work habits. They are usually written by your present or previous supervisor, manager, or team member at your request. They are used to recommend you to another employer. Employers are not obligated to write these letters and may not write them due to liability issues and company policy. If you have been a good employee, many will do so to help you obtain a new position.

If you are a student who just completed training and have little or no work experience, you can ask your instructor, internship supervisor, advisor, mentor, or volunteer coordinator to write a letter of recommendation.

If you are a person new to the labor market, with no paid work experience, it is acceptable for you to ask your landlord, neighbor, volunteer coordinator, community leader, etc., to write a letter of recommendation. It should be someone you have completed a task or project with or someone who knows you well. They need to address how long they have known you, the quality of your work or participation, dedication, skills, and work habits.

Performance Evaluation

A performance evaluation is a formal, written review or evaluation of your work. It usually covers a specific period of time and includes the quality, quantity, work habits, and attitude with which you have performed your job. It can also state your promotions, demotions, and reprimands. Positive performance evaluations can be included with your resume or application to bolster your credentials and increase your opportunities of securing a job.

CREATIVE Job Search

Job Search Tools

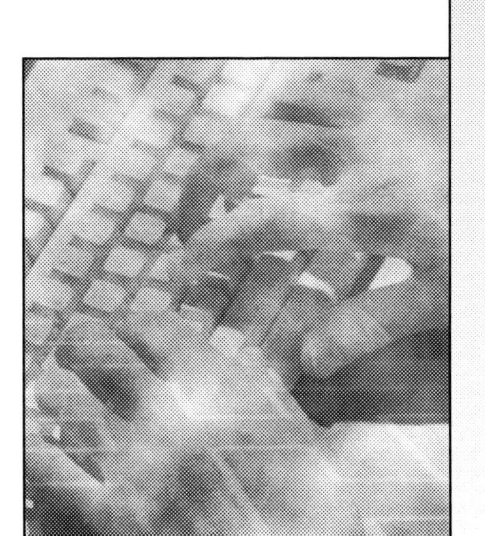

Tips

- A personal data sheet contains information you will use in your job search. Use it to refer to when completing applications, writing resumes, and to review before your interviews. Carry it with you to help you complete applications.

- Write out responses using a separate sheet of paper before completing the application. An alternative is to obtain a second application.

- Whenever possible, take the application home so you can fill it out where you are comfortable and can take your time. Read the directions carefully. It is often helpful to discuss your answers with someone else to give you perspective and direction to your responses.

- A typed application, although optional, always creates a good impression with an employer.

- Use correction fluid sparingly for fixing minor errors. Consider using a black, erasable pen or a correction ribbon on your typewriter.

- Double-check grammar, spelling, and content. When possible, ask someone to proofread it.

Job Search Tools

Personal Data Sheet

Name	
Address	

Social Security Number	Alien Card Number

Phone Numbers	Home	Fax	E-Mail

Any felony convictions?	If yes, explain:		

Employment Desired

Position Title	
Dates Available	Starting Wage
Available for Work	Full time _____ Part time _____ Temporary _____ Rotating Shifts _____ Weekend _____ On Call _____ Seasonal _____

Education

	High School	Business, Trade School, College	Undergraduate College/University	Graduate Professional
School Name				
School Location				
Years Completed	9 10 11 12	1 2 3 4	1 2 3 4	1 2 3 4
Did you graduate?		Yes No	Yes No	Yes No
Diploma/Degree				
Graduation Date				
Course of Study				
Describe any scholastic honors, assistantships, etc.				
Describe any specialized training, assistantships, etc.				
Military Training				
Foreign Languages				
Occupational License, Certifications, Registrations, Professional Affiliations, etc.				

CREATIVE Job Search

Job Search Tools

Personal Data Sheet (continued)

Employment History	List most recent employment first

Company Name/Organization

Address

Dates Employed From: Month Year To: Month Year

Job Title/Major Responsibilities/Skills, Knowledge and Abilities

Supervisor/Leader Contact? Yes No Phone

Reason for leaving Ending Salary

Company Name/Organization

Address

Dates Employed From: Month Year To: Month Year

Job Title/Major Responsibilities/Skills, Knowledge and Abilities

Supervisor/Leader Contact? Yes No Phone

Reason for leaving Ending Salary

Company Name/Organization

Address

Dates Employed From: Month Year To: Month Year

Job Title/Major Responsibilities/Skills, Knowledge and Abilities

Supervisor/Leader Contact? Yes No Phone:

Reason for leaving Ending Salary

(Other skills, knowledge, and abilities not listed above (e.g., machines operated; skilled trades; PC software; foreign or sign language). Include skills, knowledge, and abilities acquired through volunteer work, hobbies, or other interests.

CREATIVE Job Search

Job Search Tools

References

Choose your references with care. Someone who is influential in the community or business may be an effective reference, but should not be selected for this reason alone. Look for people who honestly know you and will speak objectively. Avoid references where the potential employer may assume a bias in the relationship, such as your spouse. Avoid references that may be controversial or may concern the employer. Examples of these types of references are clergy, counselors, or social workers. Of course, these are general guidelines and ultimately it is up to you to choose the best references. You may even want to use different references for different employment opportunities.

Choose your references with care.

General guidelines in selecting your references:

- When using someone as a reference, always get permission first.
- Tell them about your job search and the type of job opportunities you are seeking.
- Coach them so they will be prepared to present you as an ideal candidate.
- Find out if the reference would prefer to be contacted at work or home. Find out the best time to reach her/him. Give this information to the prospective employer.
- Be prepared to provide the reference's occupation, phone number, length of time you have known each other, and the nature of the relationship.
- Send your references a thank you note when you know they have given you a reference.
- There are four types of references (be prepared to give references from as many reference types as possible):

Employment: Includes past employers, co-workers, subordinates, or clients who can speak about your specific employment experience. You can also list the people for whom you perform volunteer activities, babysitting, lawn mowing, and other odd jobs.

Professional: People who know you on a professional basis. May include contacts from business and sales, 4-H clubs, or professional and community organizations.

Academic: Instructors and vocational counselors who can speak about your academic endeavors (appropriate for current students or recent graduates).

Personal: Neighbors and friends who know you personally and can describe your self-management skills. Doctors, librarians, bankers, and landlords may also be used as references. Use the names of people who can tell an employer you can be depended on to do a good job.

Besides preparing a list of references, you may want to secure copies of letters of recommendation from former supervisors, team members, instructors, and the like. These will be easier to obtain while you are still working or in school. However, it is possible to get them after you have left employment. Copies of written performance evaluations or grades (transcripts) from current or past employers and schools may also be helpful.

Job Search Tools

Reference Sheet

Keep this Reference Sheet with your Personal Data Sheet.

Business & Professional

Name	Company	Title	Phone Number

Personal (avoid using relatives as references)

Name	Company	Title	Phone Number

Job Search Tools

Work Samples

Jan, a hairstylist, took pictures of her customers before and after she did their hair. This convinced the employer she was capable of doing a good job and she was hired immediately.

"A picture is worth a thousand words." If this saying is true, consider the possibilities for showcasing your qualifications. Presenting a "picture" of your accomplishments using work samples will produce immediate impact and understanding of your skills.

Work samples can be presented in a variety of ways. Traditionally, artists and photographers prepare a portfolio of their best work. Video and audio tapes are used by those seeking work in the performing arts. Published works are the portfolios of journalists and reporters.

Almost every occupation lends itself to the use of work samples. A chef or baker could show photographs of culinary creations. Tailors or seamstresses could wear examples of the clothing they produced. A secretary could have a writing sample completed in school. Office support staff might present brochures, reports or newsletters as samples of their work. Pictures of auto restorations could be presented by a mechanic. Facilitators or trainers could use participant evaluations and videos of presentations. Other sources of work samples include hobbies, sports, scouts, hunting, fishing, crafts, volunteer work, and other interests.

> Almost every occupation lends itself to the use of work samples.

Work sample advantages:

Builds self-confidence: presents the tangible evidence of what you have accomplished.

Proves your credibility: shows you have the experience and can accomplish the tasks.

Proves you can do the job: overcomes the perception that you lack experience or are under qualified.

Be proactive with your work samples. While work samples may be used any time during your job search, you would usually present them at an interview. Promote the fact that you have them and want to use them to illustrate your skills, abilities, and accomplishments. After all, you are proud of what you have done. Show it!

Gene, a truck driver, built a home for his family during his free time. He did most of the work himself. When an injury forced him to find another occupation, Gene applied for a position at the "help desk" in a building supply center. Using a set of photographs his wife had taken during the construction of their house, Gene convinced the hiring manager he had the necessary knowledge and experience with building materials and tools.

Job Search Tools

NOTES

Job Search Tools

NOTES

Job Search Process

How people find work:

- Networking
- Advertised Jobs
- Agencies
- Other
- Direct Employer Contact

THE TYPICAL JOB SEARCH LOOKS SOMETHING LIKE THIS:

POSSIBLY maybe Not yet NO
Interview HOPEFULLY
2nd Interview
Delay no rejection letter
No-Response WAIT YES!

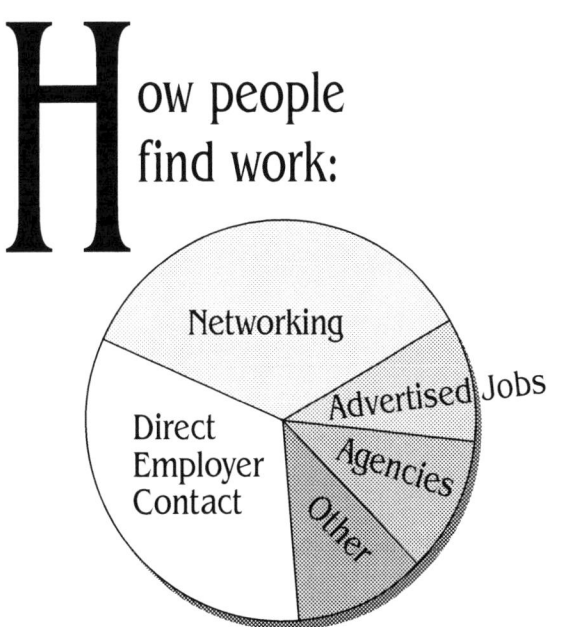

Job Search Process

Understanding how employers hire will help in planning a successful job search. Many job seekers express frustration with the hiring process. They feel a loss of control. The sense is that the employer holds all the cards and they aren't showing their hand. Knowledge is power, and understanding the hiring process is empowering. It will help direct your efforts and will eliminate some frustration.

HOW DO EMPLOYERS HIRE?

Hiring practices vary from industry to industry, employer to employer, hiring manager to hiring manager. Managers at the same employer may use a different approach. No two hiring processes are alike. However, there are a few common strategies and tools used in hiring. Recruitment, screening, and selection are three basic components of a hiring process.

Recruitment

Employers need an applicant pool from which they fill job openings. Employers who do extensive hiring may be continuously recruiting applicants, even when there is not an immediate need. They simply want to maintain the pool of applicants. Employers who hire occasionally, or for very specialized positions, will usually recruit as needed. Some employers will recruit simply to test the market. They may be planning some future expansion and want to know if they could fill their labor needs. Therefore, when employers are actively recruiting, they may not have an actual job opening.

There are many ways employers recruit applicants. Here are the most common:

Advertising: Employers may advertise in newspapers, local community papers, trade publications, radio or television, on the Internet, or on telephone job hotlines.

Internal Posting: Some employers will first post their jobs internally so interested employees may apply.

Referral: Referral from a trusted employee, colleague, or peer is the source preferred by most employers. Many employers actively solicit these referrals as part of their recruitment efforts.

Placement Service Providers: Employers may use private and public placement agencies to recruit candidates.

Personal Staffing Services: Many employers are turning to temporary and contract agencies for employee recruitment.

Job Fairs: Job fairs are an excellent source for entry-level employees. Employers who recruit at job fairs are usually building a pool of candidates and may not have an immediate opening.

Internet: Please see the following chapter on Internet Job Search.

Other Recruitment Resources: Schools, placement offices, union halls, and word of mouth.

Job Search Process

Screening

Once employers have an applicant pool, they narrow it down to the best qualified. This is no simple task. Employers are usually working with limited information. An application and/or a resume may be all they have. They may also have references and a record of past employment, but they usually will check these only after an initial screening. The reality is that for any one job, employers may have hundreds of applicants. Therefore, their first task is to eliminate as many as possible, as fast as possible. During the initial screening, employers generally spend no more than a few seconds on each application.

Employers will spend more time reviewing the small number of candidates left after an initial screening. They will look more closely at qualifications and may contact references and/or past employers. Some may call the applicant to conduct a telephone screening interview, or they may schedule an in-person screening interview. Employers are frequently turning to technology to help manage the hiring process. Growing technologies include resume scanning systems, databases, and the Internet. The goal of screening is to narrow the pool of qualified applicants to those to be interviewed.

Cindy is looking to fill a position in her department. Through a successful recruiting effort, she has 120 resumes. Cindy has one position and plans to interview no more than 10 candidates. There is no way she can thoroughly review all 120 resumes. In planning her strategy, she decides to screen the resumes for basic requirements and appearance. She quickly pages through the resumes and eliminates those that do not meet the basic requirements and those that are poorly presented or have errors. In less than an hour, Cindy has narrowed the pool of candidates down to the 10 she plans to interview.

Selection

While every step in the process plays a part in the hiring decision, employers most often make the final selection based on the interview. At the interview, employers are seeking to verify qualifications and to evaluate how the person will "fit" into the organization. When someone is called for an interview, they can be reasonably confident employers believe they are qualified for the job. Employer are interested in the person or they would not be investing their time in an interview. The question is, "Are you the best qualified person for the job?"

"Best qualified" does not just mean skills, experience, and education. Employers are also looking for motivation, a passion for excellence, and a dedication to continuous learning and quality. They are also looking at how much a new employee will cost them. Hiring is a major "purchase" that costs thousands of dollars per year. Employers want to make sure they get the best value for their money. After all, most job seekers don't come with a money-back guarantee.

The Hiring Structure

Usually, larger employers and those that do extensive hiring will have a formal hiring structure. Smaller employers and those who hire less frequently will be less formal. Also, larger employers may have several people involved in the process, while smaller employers may have one person handle the hiring. There are also industry-specific hiring practices. Medicine, education, and government are industries that have unique hiring processes. Union contracts will also influence the process.

Not everyone in the hiring process has the authority to hire. Usually one person, most often the manager of the department where the person will work, makes the final decision. If possible, it is worth finding out who will make the final decision. However, treat everyone as though they are the hiring authority. You never know who has influence on the hiring decision. At the very least, you may be working with that person if you are hired.

Job Search Process

The human resources' department is not usually the hiring authority. It manages the hiring process. Exceptions may be when hiring for an entry-level position, when the employer has many positions open, or when the position is in the human resources department. The Human Resources Department will usually recruit, screen, and schedule interviews. Although the department usually does not hire, it often has a lot of influence on the hiring decision.

> **Tom** needs to fill an opening in his department. He submits a written request to Human Resources. He includes the basic criteria for the job, how soon he needs the person, and how many candidates he wants to see. Human Resources checks the current pool of applicants and, if necessary, recruits additional candidates; screens the pool and selects the best candidates, who are referred to Tom for consideration; and schedules the interviews and processes the necessary paperwork when the decision is made.

Today's Job Market

The hiring process is more structured than it was in the past. Employers are generally more selective. Many factors have influenced the process. Large numbers of candidates, employment legislation, new technologies, employer liability, and organizational restructuring are a few of these influences. No longer do employers hire with the intent of lifetime employment. The assurance of retirement with a single employer is quickly becoming outdated. The average person will have many jobs and will change careers several times during her/his lifetime. Job search is no longer a single or rare event in life; it has become an ongoing career process. A successful job search campaign will consider these changes and will use all available resources.

Advertised Jobs

Many employers advertise their job openings. The newspapers, trade journals, television, radio, bulletin boards, grocery stores, self-service laundries, libraries, store windows, and the Internet are all sources of advertised jobs. The most common of these are newspaper advertisements. One limitation of advertised jobs is their overuse by many job seekers. Here are more limitations of advertised jobs:

- Because they are seen by more job seekers, the competition is much greater.
- They represent only a small percentage of available jobs. Most employers prefer to use other sources for recruiting candidates.
- Many are "fake" openings. There is no real job, or the opening has already been filled. Employers may advertise to test the market, while some are required to advertise because of Equal Employment Opportunity requirements or Federal contracting.
- Some are undesirable jobs. They may pay low wages or the employer may have trouble keeping employees.

Despite this, there are many good jobs to be found through advertisements. Employers needing specialized skills and those who are mass recruiting (seeking to fill many positions) will often advertise. Also, advertisements are excellent windows into the job market; they are one measure of growth industries. Here are some tips for advertised jobs:

- Actively look for advertised jobs, but do not make them your primary focus.
- Pick your sources for advertised jobs— newspapers, trade journals, the Internet, etc., then follow them faithfully. Review new listings when they are released.
- Respond to new openings immediately.
- Keep track of listings that run continuously or are old. Review past advertisements to see which jobs have been listed before.
- Don't ignore "blind" ads (ads where you apply to a box number and do not know the employer's name). Many good jobs are listed as blind ads.
- Look at all the jobs listed, not just those that fit your goal. You may find an employer you want to pursue even though a job in your occupation is not listed.
- Research the employer and the job before you apply.
- Direct your application to a person by name. Avoid "To whom it may concern" or "Personnel Manager."
- When you apply, attempt to meet the hiring authority. Don't just send your resume or application and wait.
- After you apply, follow-up with the employer. Check with the employer often; ask for an interview; show your initiative.

Job Search Process

NETWORKING

Employment experts agree that most job openings are never advertised.

Jan and Frank moved so now they need a family doctor. Frank asks his co-workers while Jan checks with the neighbors for referrals to a good doctor.

Kevin is having car trouble and does not know where to have it fixed. He calls a couple of people at school to ask if they can suggest someone.

Mary is asked to travel out-of-state for work, but is not sure about the paperwork. She solicits help from a colleague who has recently traveled out-of-state.

Gene is building a scale model of a fire station for his 5th grade class. He calls the local fire department and arranges to meet with the captain to work out the details.

Sue was looking for her first job as a receptionist. While she was attending a Minnesota WorkForce Center job club, another participant told her about an opening where his wife works.

Each of these people has something in common; they are all networking. Wherever there are communities and civilizations, there is networking. What has changed over time is how networking occurs. In the past, networking was informal and random. In fact, most people didn't even know that they were networking. Today networking has become calculated and structured. People network every day without thinking about it. However, more people are including formal networking as part of their daily activities.

Most employers don't need to advertise. There are enough applicants available to them without advertising. Also, most employers don't want to advertise. They would rather consider someone referred to them from a trusted employee or colleague. It's like looking for a doctor or an auto mechanic; most people would rather go to someone recommended rather than to a name found in an advertisement. If this is the case, then how does someone find these jobs? Direct employer contact and networking are the answers.

Formal networking is the systematic pursuit of new contacts and information. It is organized and planned. Networking is relational. A good networking relationship will be mutually beneficial to both parties. Many people have trouble with formal networking, especially as a job search strategy.

Here are some common networking concerns:

"I'm embarrassed to admit that I'm looking for work."

"I feel that it would be like begging for a job."

"I don't want people to think that I'm taking advantage of them."

Now let's dismiss each of these concerns:

- Looking for work does not carry the stigma that it did in the past. The average person will change jobs every five years. Your networking contacts will be much more sympathetic than you may think.

- Networking is not begging. In fact, you should not be asking for a job; you should be seeking information that may lead to a job. Usually your networking contacts will not be potential employers—they will be people who know about potential employment. If you discover that a contact is a potential employer, take off your networking hat and pursue employment.

- Good networking is a mutually beneficial relationship. Plan to give as much or more than you receive. Also, you will be surprised at how willing people are to help. In fact, they will be honored that you value their input.

CREATIVE Job Search 100

Job Search Process

Networking Strategies

Networking strategies range from basic to sophisticated. Here are some general networking ideas.

- Do not just wait to bump into people. Initiate contacts for the sole purpose of networking.

- Develop a networking list. Make contact with each person on your list. Add names of people you meet or are referred to by your contacts.

- Set networking goals. Write down specific goals for how many networking contacts you plan to make each week. Regularly check your progress.

- Set goals for each meeting. Don't just get together and see where it leads; meet with a purpose. Express this goal when you arrange the meeting.

- Come to the meeting prepared. Know what questions you want to ask. Take notes.

- Always ask if the person knows of anyone else you should meet. Ask if you can use her/his name when contacting the person.

- Maintain networking files. Keep a record of the outcomes of each contact and important information about the person.

- Meet in person whenever possible.

- Let the person know you value his/her information and professional opinion.

- Plan your follow-up. At the time you meet with someone, plan when you will contact this person again. Write it down on a follow-up calendar.

- If you agree to do something for someone, be sure to follow through.

- Say "thank you" often. Send a thank you letter or card.

The Networking Campaign

There are four basic categories of networking contacts. Each has its own unique value. A good networking campaign will draw from each category.

1. **People you know well: friends, family, neighbors, and co-workers.**

    This is a good place to begin your networking campaign. These people have the most interest in your success and are excellent networking contacts. These are the people with whom you are most comfortable and from whom you can ask for the most assistance. However, when networking with this group, set clear goals. They may want to help more than you wish. Acknowledge their value and say "thank you." This group is often the least appreciated.

2. **People you see occasionally: acquaintances, or business contacts.**

    More than 25 percent of the people who find jobs through networking received the referral from someone they see once a year or less! These are people with whom you may feel less comfortable with, but they also have the greatest potential. Ask this group for ideas and referrals. You may need to reintroduce yourself. State your purpose, acknowledge their value, and request a meeting. It is a good idea to set reasonable time limits for the meeting. Let them know you only want 30 minutes of their time. Be sure you stick to your time limit. Come well prepared, and be professional and organized in your discussion.

3. **Referrals from your other networking contacts.**

    Stretch your network by meeting new people who are the friends, associates, and acquaintances of your networking contacts. Sometimes these will be people with additional information, but they may also be potential employers. In either case, review the sections on Direct Employer Contact, page 103, and Telephone Communications, page 104. Most job seekers will now be out of their comfort zone. This is where you will find the real action. You are getting closer to that job. When approaching a referral contact, introduce yourself with a lead statement that will get their attention. Use the name of the person who referred you. State your purpose and request a meeting. You should also limit the time for the meeting, be well prepared, and be professional.

4. **Cold calling people you do not know and to whom you have not been referred.**

    Through your employment research and networking, you may discover the names of people with whom you would like to talk. This type of contact takes another level of confidence, but the potential is great. Take the initiative and you will find that these contacts will pay off.

CREATIVE Job Search

Job Search Process

Networking List

Here is a list to get you started.

- Friends
- Neighbors
- Social acquaintances— bridge group, hiking club, softball team, etc.
- Social club members
- Health club members
- PTA members or groups
- Classmates— from any level of school
- College alumni— get a list of those living in the area
- Teachers— your teachers, professors, your children's
- Anybody you wrote a check to in the last year
- Drugstore owner
- Doctor, dentist, optician
- Lawyer, accountant, real estate agent
- Insurance agent, stockbroker, travel agent
- Veterinarian
- Dry cleaner
- Flower shop owner or manager/sales clerks
- Manager of your local bank
- Current and former co-workers
- Relatives
- Politicians
- Chamber of Commerce executives
- Professional association executives
- Trade association executives
- Members of professional organizations
- Religious leaders— check your fellowship/congregation for a job-loss support group
- Members of your fellowship/parish/church/congregation/synagogue
- People you meet at conventions
- Speakers at meetings you've attended
- Business club executives and members— Rotary, Kiwanis, Jaycees, etc.
- Friends you served with in the military
- Volunteer affiliations
- Friends of your parents
- People you meet on airplanes, riding the bus (you never know!)
- Community meetings
- Daycare facilities
- YMCA/YWCA
- Coaches
- Mechanics
- Hairdresser/barber
- Other _____
- Other _____

Networking Log

It is important to document and follow-up all job leads. Use this sheet for keeping track of all your networking activity. Always ask if they will suggest another contact. Keep the ball rolling!

Contact Name _____ Date Called _____

Company Name _____

Address _____

Action Plan _____

Fax _____ Appointment Date/Time _____

E-Mail Address _____

Summary of Conversation/Contact _____

Special Interests/Proud Accomplishments
of Person Interviewed _____

Follow-up _____

Contact Names Received (List below new leads from this contact)

Name _____	Name _____
Position _____	Position _____
Employer _____	Employer _____
Phone _____	Phone _____
Fax/E-Mail _____	Fax/E-Mail _____

Job Search Process

DIRECT EMPLOYER CONTACT

A goal of a job search campaign is to meet face-to-face with employers (interviews). The more interviews you have, the greater your chances for success. If you are not getting interviews, it is unlikely that you will have job offers. Most job seekers prefer a passive job search strategy. They submit an application or resume and wait. When they don't hear anything, they repeat the process. On the other hand, successful job seekers are proactive in their approach. They take the initiative to make direct contact with potential employers. Contacting employers directly is fundamental to a successful job search.

Direct employer contact requires preparation, confidence, and persistence. Many people are uncomfortable with this approach. They are afraid that they will offend the employer and hurt their chances for employment. A certain amount of concern is healthy; it is important to be considerate of employers and respect their time. But also remember that you have something they need. You're not asking for a handout— you are selling a quality product! If you don't take the initiative, no one will take it for you.

Direct employer contact works for advertised jobs. Even if an advertised job discourages direct contact, it is to your advantage to take the initiative. A wise policy is to first follow the advertised directions, then make direct contact. If the advertisement states, "Send a resume," send your resume, then follow it with a phone call.

Direct contact is the logical conclusion to a successful networking campaign. As your networking pays off in referrals to employers, you will have to make direct contacts. You have the advantage of using the name of your referral to soften the contact.

Michael found a position in the newspaper that discouraged direct contact. Determined to do more that just send his resume, Michael researched the employer, then called and asked for an interview. Not only was he granted the interview, he subsequently won the job. To top this, Michael was not skilled in sales or a polished communicator. Michael had a severe speech impediment and was partially paralyzed.

You will also want to make direct contact with employers who are not advertising and to whom you have not been referred. This is called cold calling. Cold calling is difficult for many people, but it is an extremely productive job search strategy.

Press on! Nothing in the world can take the place of persistence.

Basic Principles of Direct Employer Contact

- Preparation is critical to success. Research the employer, the industry, and the job.
- Direct contact may be in-person or by phone. However, the ultimate goal is an in-person interview.
- The goal is to present your qualifications directly to the hiring manager.
- The goal is not to talk with the Human Resources Department, unless you are looking for a job in the department or it is the hiring authority. Respect the Human Resources Department by complying with the hiring process.
- The goal is not to submit an application or resume. If an application or resume is requested, graciously comply and continue your direct contact.
- When you make direct contact, do not begin by asking if they are hiring, or by saying you are unemployed. Capture their attention with your qualifications and ask for an interview.
- Plan your follow-up. If you are granted an interview, this is your next step. Otherwise come to an agreement with the employer about when you will call back.
- Sell your qualifications, send your resume, and plan your follow-up even if an employer is not hiring. You never know what will happen tomorrow.
- Whenever possible, the next step is your responsibility— not the employer's. For example, if an employer says, "We will call you in a couple of weeks," you could respond with, "Would it be all right if I call you two weeks from today?" If they say "Yes," then you have agreed on your follow-up and the responsibility is yours.
- Expect rejection! It goes with the territory. Don't take rejection personally.
- Maintain a good attitude and a healthy sense of humor.

103 CREATIVE Job Search

Job Search Process

TELEPHONE COMMUNICATIONS

Not many people can imagine a world without telephones. They have become a fundamental part of our lives. Telephone communications have advanced to a degree of sophistication few people could have ever imagined. Telemarketing, voice mail, conference calling, e-mail, and fax machines have all added to this revolution.

The telephone is a critical tool in a successful job search campaign. It is almost guaranteed that you will talk to a potential employer on the telephone at some point in the hiring process. Shrewd job seekers use advanced telephone marketing techniques in their job search. They use the telephone to make direct employer contact and to open the doors of opportunity. The telephone is a powerful tool in presenting your qualifications to an employer. Effective telephone techniques are critical skills all job seekers need.

Good telephone communication requires skills— skills that can be learned. Just because someone talks on the telephone a lot does not mean they are effective communicators. In fact, many people who use the telephone frequently have mastered some very offensive habits. It is never too early or too late to learn good telephone communications. Telephone skills are marketable job skills many employers value.

In a comprehensive job search, you will be using the telephone to conduct research, cold call employers, make networking contacts, schedule meetings, and to interview. Using the telephone is an efficient and effective use of your time and resources. The telephone can get you behind closed doors which will help you contact those hard-to-reach people.

Scripting

Preparation is critical to good telephone communication. It is not wise to call someone and just start talking. This may work for family and friends, but it will kill a job search. Telephone communications in a job search campaign are business calls, not personal calls. Actually, they are sales calls. Some people have a hard time with the idea of telephone sales. None of us likes a pushy telemarketer. But many of the same concepts and strategies that go into telephone sales go into your job search campaign. A business or sales caller has about 20 seconds to capture the hearer's attention. Therefore, communication has to be to the point and concise. There is no time to wander. Scripting is the answer.

Scripting is simply planning what you are going to say. Most people script important conversations; they just don't realize that is what they are doing. Have you ever made an important call and found yourself hesitating to dial the last number? Or hanging up before you are finished dialing? You were probably scripting in your mind what you were going to say. You may want to take it a step further and write down what you plan to say. That is what skilled telemarketers do; they have a script they follow.

Job Search Process

Basic Principles of Scripting

- Have an objective for the call. You may be seeking information, trying to schedule a meeting, or presenting your qualifications to a potential employer.

- Have a secondary objective. Often you will not achieve your primary objective, but every telephone call is an opportunity to solicit information.

- Know the name of the person to whom you wish to speak. If you do not know the person's name, then obtaining it becomes your first objective.

- Outline in writing what you want to say. This is important in the early stages of cold calling or when the call is very important. Later on, you will script most of your calls in your head. Do not read your script. Your presentation should be natural.

- The script will depend on the goal of the call and whether you know the person you are calling. A good script should include the following:

Introduction: Tell the person who you are.

Lead statement: Make a quick statement designed to get the person's attention.

Body: State your purpose for the call.

Close: Accomplish your goal, ask for information, schedule the meeting, etc.

Script for Contact Information

Caller: "Hi. This is Jerry Job. I am trying to contact the person in charge of marketing. Who would that be?"

Receiver: "That is John Smith. He is the director."

Caller: "I need to contact him about some marketing concerns. Does he have a direct number or an extension number?"

Receiver: "His direct number is 555-5555. Would you like me to transfer you?"

Script for Follow-up Information

Caller: "Hello. This is Jerry Job. I interviewed for the computer programmer position last week. I am just checking to see if the hiring decision has been made."

Receiver: "Not yet. We anticipate making our final selection this Wednesday."

Caller: "I'm still very interested in the position. You're doing some very innovative multimedia work that's on the cutting edge of today's technology. Best of all, you have a bright and energetic technical staff that understands the importance of team production. I'm sure we would work well together. Would it be okay if I called you on Wednesday? What would be the best time?"

Job Search Process

Basic Principles of Telephone Communications

- **Practice**—Telephone skills, like all skills, have to be practiced to be mastered. Start with low-risk calls. Practice your presentation with a friend and read your script out loud.

- **Voice Mail**—Whether you like it or not, voice mail is a part of our lives. Speaking to a machine adds a new dimension to telephone skills. When you get voice mail, listen carefully to the message so you can comply with the instructions. It is a good idea to know what you will say before you make your call. Having a script ready will enable you to leave a message that is upbeat, simple, clear, and concise. Your message should be 30 seconds or less. It is amazing how an otherwise skilled telephone user comes across as monotone and unsure on a message machine. If you have an answering machine, make sure your message is polite and professional, and be sure you answer your messages.

- **Location**—Call from a quiet place where you can concentrate. Do not call from a noisy restaurant, bus station, street corner, or when the kids are yelling or the dog is barking.

- **Organization**—Have all your job search materials nearby and take notes.

- **Listen Carefully**—Communication is what is said, how it's said, and the body language that is used. It is important to listen carefully to what you are saying, how you are saying it, and how you are being received. If you sense you have called at a bad time, politely ask if there is a better time. It may be useful to tape record yourself while conducting a simulated call.

- **"Buy" Signals**—A "buy" signal is evidence that you have captured the person's attention. "Buy" signals usually take the form of questions. When someone is asking questions about your qualifications, they are, for the moment, interested in you.

- **Objections**—Objections come in many forms. "We are looking for someone with more experience or education," or "Sorry, we're not hiring right now." Press on to your goal and continue to sell your qualifications. Look for ways to eliminate the objection.

- **Follow-up**—It is the persistent 20 percent who make 80 percent of the sales! The best time to plan a follow-up is when you make the contact. While you have the contact on the telephone, agree on when you will call back. Keep a follow-up calendar and maintain a record of your contacts. If you agree to call back, be sure to do so. If someone agrees to call you, state the best time to be reached. The last thing you want to do is sit by the telephone waiting for a call that may never come.

Additional Telephone Tips

- Wear a smile on the telephone—they may not see it but they will hear it.

- Dress for making telephone contacts as you would for an interview. Your professionalism and preparation will be heard (you may also be asked to come right down).

- If you can't get past a shrewd receptionist, try before 8:00 a.m., during lunch, after 5:00 p.m., or Saturday morning. If you still can't get through, solicit the receptionist's assistance.

- Look for ways to compliment the person or the company.

- Don't apologize for making the contact. You have a product they need and a right to present yourself.

- Don't sell yourself from a position of weakness or apologize for what you do not have or have not done. Sell yourself from a position of strength and stress those skills, attributes, and accomplishments attractive to the employer.

THE TYPICAL JOB SEARCH LOOKS SOMETHING LIKE THIS:

POSSIBLY maybe Not Yet NO interview HOPEFULLY 2nd Interview rejection letter Delay no No Response WAIT YES! cancelled meeting wait some more

CREATIVE Job Search

Job Search Process

Telephone Preparation Form

Date: _____

Contact person
(full name and title): _____

Employer name: _____

Address: _____

Telephone number(s): _____

Script

Primary goal: _____

Secondary goal: _____

Introduction: _____
_____
_____

Lead statement: _____
_____
_____

Body: _____
_____
_____

Conclusion: _____
_____
_____

Results/Comments: _____
_____
_____

Follow-up action to be taken: _____
_____
_____

Job Search Process

PERSONNEL STAFFING SERVICES

Personnel staffing services can be an excellent job search resource. They are sometimes known as contract or search firms, or employment agencies. They offer a variety of services and options for the job seeker. These firms can be private, public, for profit, or nonprofit. Some specialize in service to specific groups of people and have eligibility requirements; others serve the general public. Each firm is unique and may provide a combination of blended services. The type of services offered may be influenced by whom they represent— you or the employer. Generally, their focus is on matching your skills with the job openings of employers or companies. Depending on your circumstances and needs, many of them can be of benefit in helping you look for and secure employment. Therefore, it is important to assess your situation, know what you want and need from the firm, know the services they offer, and clearly understand both the firm's and your rights and responsibilities.

Types of service offered may vary. Here is a description of common services:

Staffing/Recruiting. Employers use staffing services to assist them in filling their job openings. In some instances, they recruit, perform extensive interviewing, check references, and submit only the most qualified applicants to the employer. Some staffing services are primarily a bulletin board service where job orders and/or resumes are posted, and you or the employer may contact each other.

Job Search Training. Some staffing services offer specific training in job search skills. This can help you develop valuable skills to enable you to successfully find your own job. This training may include individual workshops and materials on a variety of job search topics. Some firms specialize in resume writing, although sometimes there is a fee for this service. Be sure to find out before requesting this service.

Career Counseling and Planning. If you are looking for a job or entering the labor market for the first time, it is beneficial to talk with a career counselor to help you with self-assessment, knowledge of the labor market, employment trends, and training opportunities. Some firms employ career counselors or advisors who provide these services. They usually offer aptitude, interest, personality, and skill testing to help you with career changes and to fulfill your potential by matching you to employment opportunities.

Outplacement or Career Transition. When companies downsize their workforce, some firms will provide laid-off employees with outplacement assistance. This can include: job search workshops and materials, phone rooms, job leads, resume design, job club, and employment counseling. Ask your employer if these services will be provided.

Temporary and Contract Employment. These are firms that refer you to temporary employment opportunities as requested by an employer who specifies the job requirements and time period of the work assignment. Usually, you are working for the temporary or contract firm during this time and are paid by them. Some employers use this means to try out new employees and may hire you later if you have performed well and they have a job opening. Others only have a short-term or seasonal need that is best met through this service.

Job Search Process

Benefits

The benefit to you, the job seeker, can be varied and many. You can build skills and meet financial needs while continuing to look for work. It is easier to get a job when you have a job. You may be able to get more flexible hours or working conditions to accommodate your personal situation. Some staffing services offer transportation, testing, training, child care, medical, and other benefits. This type of employment can also be useful for those who need to gain work experience, develop skills, obtain training, or increase networking contacts. It is also a good way to check out a company or an occupation before making a commitment to training, a particular career, or a particular company.

Tips to Consider

- Job seekers working with personnel staffing services need to be wise consumers. Check into the firm's reputation. Use the ones that are going to best meet your present and future employment needs. Determine if any fees will be charged for services before accepting or signing anything.

- Staffing services work with the job market daily, and can provide valuable information that is helpful in your job search. In all dealings, treat them as you would treat a potential employer. They represent a variety of companies and can expose you to many opportunities that are otherwise not available.

- Take ownership of your own career and job search. Do not assume if you are working with a staffing service that you can sit back and wait. Use as many resources as possible to help you achieve your goal.

- Temporary staffing services are your employers when you are on assignment for them. Ask about items you need to know before you agree to accept employment. Those items could include: pay rate, benefits, estimated length of assignment, the chance of becoming an employee of the company, and what is expected of you. Also, let them know the hours and days you are available, your overtime availability, transportation, and salary needs.

- Consider the secondary objectives of any service you are thinking of using. An example might be career counseling provided by training or educational institutions. They may have a primary interest in enrolling you in their training program for funding reasons. Be sure to check out their placement rates and services with the Department of Education, Better Business Bureau, or with former students.

- If you are receiving Unemployment Insurance benefits, know the effect of short-term wages and the consequences of turning down job opportunities. Short-term wages may affect eligibility and benefit amounts. They may also extend the length of time that benefits can be received.

Personnel staffing services offer a variety of services and options for the job seeker.

Job Search Process

NOTES

Internet Job Search Strategies

"Never assume the way you've always job hunted is a sure thing."

From *Electronic Job Search Revolution,*
Joyce Lain Kennedy and Thomas J. Morrow

Internet Job Search Strategies

The Internet is changing the way we communicate and receive information. Not since the telephone (and possibly the printing press) has technology created such a widespread impact on civilization. Many experts believe that the Internet will become as widely used and accepted as the telephone or the television. It may become so necessary to business and society that people will be helpless without it.

The Internet combines people and computers to form a global network of information, communication, and community. The Internet is an electronic community with its own culture and subculture. It has its own rules of behavior and etiquette (netiquette). Nearly everything found in a physical community (businesses, social organizations, government agencies, educational institutions, and individuals) can also be found in cyberspace. Every idea, ideology, and interest is represented. Exploring the Internet is much like maneuvering through life. The challenge is to master the technologies and the culture.

This chapter is not intended to teach you all there is to know about the Internet. It assumes you have a basic knowledge of computers and the means to access the Internet. This entails a computer (at least the use of one), a software program called the "browser," and an Internet provider (to get you access to the Internet). Just about any computer you can purchase today will have a browser pre-loaded on it. Contacting a service provider is the next logical step. In Minnesota, the WorkForce Centers have computers you can use at no charge for much of what will be discussed in this chapter. You may also find computers at libraries, schools, and retail establishments that may or may not charge you for use.

THE INTERNET JOB SEARCH

A successful job search requires a variety of skills, tools, and strategies. There is no one factor that brings success. It is the combination of many individual efforts. The Internet is a gold mine of employment resources. For every major job search strategy there is an Internet counterpart. If you are serious about your job search, it's worth your time to explore these resources.

The fundamental tool for finding information on the Internet is the search engine. Search engines use keywords to locate web pages, listings in electronic directories, or messages in newsgroups. Some engines search the Internet in general while others search a specific site. Mastering these tools is critical to effectively and efficiently locating information on the Internet.

There are many search sites on the Internet. Each one is a little different in its focus and use. To learn how to use a specific search engine, look for the "help" feature. Most search tools provide instruction on their use.

Internet job search resources include:
- Job postings
- Resume posting
- Job search assistance
- Information on employers, occupations, industries, and employment
- Access to people important to your success
- Telephone and business directories
- Customized maps that help with your travel
- Automation that notifies you when a job matches your interests

You can use the Internet to distribute your resume, make direct contact with potential employers, and follow up on job leads.

The Internet does not replace traditional job search strategies. Few people today can conduct an effective job search using only the Internet. Pen and paper applications, paper resumes, direct contact with potential employers, face-to-face networking, and interviewing are still fundamental. However, the use of technology has also become essential to a successful job search. The goal is to win a face-to-face meeting with an employer. In the near future, that face-to-face interview may be conducted by video conference from the comfort of your home.

There is a danger of relying too much on technical methods. It's likely you will find time on the Internet more fun than job search. Many job search activities push us beyond our comfort zone. Beware of those who promote an easy job search. The most effective strategies, traditional or technical, require work. A serious job search is still a full-time job.

Internet Job Search Strategies

Employment Research

Information is a critical part of a successful job search and is obtained through research. You'll want to learn as much as possible about potential employers, your occupation, and your industry. There is no such thing as having too much information in a job search. Information is power. Information gives you control and confidence.

Benefits of Research
- Increased control and confidence
- Focuses your efforts
- Better time management
- Minimizes wasted efforts
- Improved resumes and cover letters
- Attracts the attention of more employers
- Confidence and improved performance in interviews
- Improved decision making
- Strengthens your ability to negotiate the best job offer
- Increased potential for job search success
- Greater potential for job satisfaction and economic security
- Successfully compete with other job seekers
- Improved potential for success once you start a new job

Prior to the Internet, employment research meant spending a lot of time at the library gathering and studying books, periodicals, articles, and business literature. It also meant attending professional meetings, networking, and going to informational interviews. While the Internet has not eliminated any of these activities, it has made many of them easier.

Electronic Directories

Printed directories are a common source of information. They provide basic information, usually organized alphabetically by topic. One example of a directory is the phone book Yellow Pages. The Internet is an excellent way to access directories. All of the phone books in the United States are published on the web. This is very useful for people looking to relocate. It is also useful when conducting a local job search. Directory listings on the Internet often contain more information than their paper versions. Along with the address, there may be a map showing where the organization is located. You may be provided the option to enter your location and obtain specific travel directions. The listing may contain a link to the organization's website where more information is available.

There are directories designed specifically for the Internet such as the popular site Yahoo. Its "address" on the Internet is **www.yahoo.com** There are directories that specialize in a specific subject or geographic region. The "links" pages found on most websites are also a type of directory. These can be very useful because they have been reviewed and recommended by someone else interested in the subject.

Linda just completed training as a nursing assistant and is looking for potential employers. She decided the best way to start would be to look for nursing home names and addresses in the phone book. At a local library she was able to access phone books on the Internet. With little effort, she found a list of nursing homes in her area, along with maps to their locations and links to their websites. Linda followed one of the links and found a nursing home that was nearby. There she found information about the facility and also found a list of job openings. She also found the name, phone number, and e-mail address for the assistant director of nursing responsible for hiring nursing assistants.

You'll want to learn as much as possible about potential employers, your occupation, and your industry.

Internet Job Search Strategies

On-line Magazines and Newspapers

On the Internet you can access a lot of published information. Most magazines and newspapers are also published on the Internet. You have access to thousands of free local and worldwide publications. If you are looking to relocate, you can find publications from distant communities. The search capabilities of the Internet make finding information fast and efficient. How long would it take you to go through one magazine or an average-size newspaper and find every occurrence of the word "healthcare?" Not just in the titles of articles, but anywhere in the publication? How long would it take to search a stack of publications or a whole room full of publications? While the search capabilities of each website will vary, many sites give you the power to search an archive of issues in a matter of seconds. Most sites provide the ability to search at least their current publication.

Lang is an electronic technician with the U.S. Army stationed in Japan. He will be released from military service soon and plans to return to his home in Minnesota. Lang has been researching the local job market through newspapers published on the Internet. He uses the search features of these publications to find articles of specific interest. From his research, Lang learned about the local economy and identified several potential employers. He has further researched employers by browsing their websites and made initial contact by e-mail. When Lang returns to Minnesota, he will be well on his way to landing an excellent civilian job.

Chuck is a welder with limited work experience. He recently applied for an entry-level job with a local manufacturing company. The company telephoned Chuck and scheduled an interview. At a Creative Job Search seminar, Chuck learned that he should research an employer when preparing for an interview. Chuck went to his local Minnesota WorkForce Center where he found public access to the Internet. Within a few minutes, Chuck had located the company's website. There he learned more than he expected. The next day at the interview the first question was, "What do you know about what we do?" The interviewer was visibly impressed with Chuck's knowledge and obvious preparation. Chuck got the job. He was also given a higher starting wage than was originally stated.

Websites

Many organizations publish a website that supports their business. The web is growing very fast. New sites are being created every day. In the near future, it will be standard practice for organizations to have a website. It will become as common as business cards and listings in the phone book. The quantity, quality, and type of information found on a website will vary. At a minimum, you should learn about their location, products, or services. You may also find vision and mission statements, a history of the organization, names of key employees, business plans, and much more.

In addition to employer websites, there are many other sites that provide useful information.

Employment research sites include:
- Professional Associations
- Research Organizations
- Government Agencies
- Educational Institutions
- Community Organizations
- Libraries

The best tools for locating websites are search engines and directories. Search on the name of the site or use topical and geographic keywords. There are many directories you can use to find sites.

When viewing websites, consider the source and relevance of the information. If the research will have a significant impact on an important decision, look for ways to verify the information. Consider who authored the information and its timeliness. Look for other sources that agree with the information.

Internet Job Search Strategies

Nancy received a voice message from an employer who found her resume in the Minnesota Job Bank. The only information the employer left was his name, the name of the company, and a phone number. Typically, Nancy would have called the employer without having any background information. She would have learned what she needed to know during the phone call. Instead, Nancy spent 15 minutes on the Internet researching the employer. She found the employer's website that outlined its business, mission, vision, and history. She also found an article about the employer. When Nancy returned the telephone call, she had valuable information that helped her to effectively communicate her qualifications and evaluate the employment opportunity.

Carlos is considering changing careers. He has identified the paralegal occupation as one in which he has an interest. He has read a lot of published information on the paralegal occupation. Carlos researched the National Paralegal Association Website on the Internet, but it was not enough. He wanted to talk directly with people who were currently working as paralegals to hear their personal perspective and experience. Carlos did not know anyone in the local chapter of the Paralegal Association. With the help of the website DejaNews (**www.dejanews.com**), Carlos was able to locate Internet newsgroups where there were discussions relating to paralegals. Carlos subscribed to a couple of groups and began reading the posts and listening to the discussions (also known as "lurking"). He eventually posted a message introducing himself and describing his interests. In a short time, Carlos learned more than he expected. He was provided advice on training programs, employment trends and how to succeed in the paralegal profession.

Electronic Networking

Would you like to network with professionals in your industry, from all over the world without traveling great distances to attend expensive conferences? Looking for another way to make direct contact with potential employers? In cyberspace you can! The Internet is a networker's paradise.

The Internet provides access to people from all over the world. The challenge is to find the person with the information you are seeking. Electronic networking uses three basic Internet tools— news groups, e-mail, and "live" chat. To master these tools requires specialized communication skills. To be successful in this media requires preparation and practice. Many of the standards that apply to good telephone communication apply to the Internet.

Websites, Internet publications, and directories are excellent sources of information. However, frequently the information you need is not published. Some of the best insight comes from the personal experience and knowledge of individuals. A great deal of insight can be gained by reading published information about an employer or occupation. But a very different kind of insight is gained by talking to someone who works for that employer or in that occupation.

Effectively communicating electronically is both a science and a culture. It involves technology and society. The Internet community has its own culture and etiquette (netiquette). Mastering these communications is a rewarding challenge. It will open up a new world of opportunity. To learn about electronic communication, go to **www.learnthenet.com**

Tips for Internet Research

Be Focused. Using the Internet for research is not the same as "surfing" the Internet. It can be compared to taking a Sunday drive versus purchasing tires for your car. On a Sunday drive you can wander wherever the road leads. In fact, the less planned, the greater the adventure. On the other hand, you would not just wander around until you found a tire store. Stay focused on your research goal. If you find something interesting en route to your goal, "bookmark" the site and come back to it. It would be like finding a candy store on your way to get tires. Before you know it, you have lost track of what you wanted to accomplish.

Develop a Research Strategy. Develop a plan before you begin looking for information. Decide in advance how much time you are willing to invest. Your topic will influence where you look. The World Wide Web, newsgroups, and e-mail all require a different search strategy. Knowing roughly where your information might be found will help in developing your plan. Remember, "Plan your work, then work your plan."

Keep Records. Whether it's websites, computer files, or paper files, it is important to keep a record of your research. As you explore potential employers, industries, and communities, you will collect a lot of information. Discard that which has little or no immediate value, then file and maintain information that you want to keep. Almost every Internet newbie has given in to the temptation to bookmark sites without discretion. The result is almost always an unmanageable tangle of Internet bookmarks.

Set Goals. Goals will help keep you on track and should be stated in specific terms. "I'm going to spend the next hour researching two potential employers who might need someone with marketing skills," is far better stated than, "I'm going to look for jobs on the Internet."

Internet Job Search Strategies

ELECTRONIC COMMUNICATIONS

Communication is fundamental to a successful job search. You could say that job search is communication. Consider the topics found in the Creative Job Search guide.

Communication is at the heart of these topics:
- Skills Identification
- Resumes and Cover Letters
- Employment Applications
- Reasons for Leaving
- References
- Work Samples
- Networking
- Direct Employer Contact
- Telephone Communications
- The Job Interview
- Thank you Letters
- Negotiating Tips
- Job Success Skills

E-mail

A very successful job search strategy is to make direct contact with a potential employer. It can also be very difficult. First, you have to identify the person. Then, you have to find the best way to make contact. The telephone is a popular tool for this purpose. Speaking on the telephone is an art, and it is sometimes difficult to connect with a person by phone. E-mail is an excellent alternative. It gives you access to the individual any time of the day or night (whenever they read their messages). It also offers greater control over your message. On the phone it's easy to say the wrong thing or say it in the wrong way. With e-mail you can edit and refine your message until it says exactly what you want.

E-mail can also be used to follow-up after an interview, communicate with networking contacts, references, and placement professionals, and for sending your resume and thank you note. E-mail is a powerful and unique communication tool. It is not as formal as a business letter, but it is more formal than a phone call. E-mail is most effective when communicating with people who actively use e-mail. Many people who have e-mail don't use it and may prefer other forms of communication. Whenever possible, find out early the person's preference for communication. Making first contact with a stranger, especially a potential employer, is always a challenge. But it is also very necessary to an effective job search. When making first contact with someone by e-mail, be very polite and professional. Introduce yourself with something of interest to the reader. You want to capture their attention and interest. Don't just say "Hi, my name is Joe and I'm looking for a job." Communicate what you want from the reader. Be specific— you are looking for information or you would like to schedule a meeting. Finish with your intent to follow-up and an alternative way the person can contact you. If you do not receive a reply, and you are serious about making contact, try a different form of communication (call them on the phone).

Frank submitted his resume to an employer for consideration. He attempted to follow-up directly with the employer by phone to discuss his qualifications and schedule a meeting. However, the employer was never available. Frank left messages on voice mail and with the receptionist. With the help of a directory on the web, Frank was able to locate the employer's e-mail address. He sent the employer a message introducing himself and initiated a discussion. The employer promptly responded, asking more about Frank's experience. A series of e-mail messages was sent between Frank and the employer. The final result was the employer hired Frank.

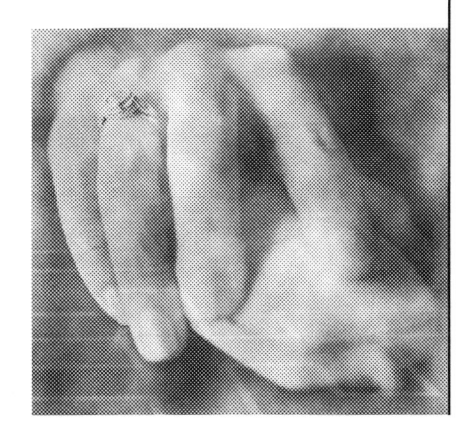

Internet Job Search Strategies

Good electronic communication is not just being able to retrieve, browse or send messages.

Tips for Electronic Communication:

- Keep messages short and concise.
- Check for proper spelling, grammar, and punctuation.
- Say exactly what you mean.
- Give your message a descriptive and enticing subject.
- When replying to someone else's message, include or summarize the original message.
- AVOID USING ALL CAPITAL LETTERS. In electronic communication it is the equivalent of shouting.
- Many people regard *emoticons* :-) as unprofessional. Use them sparingly.
- Avoid acronyms (e.g., BTW— by the way, IMHO— in my humble opinion).
- In heated messages, respond to the subject, not the individual. If you are angry, wait several hours or a day to respond.
- Always be courteous and professional.
- If you send e-mail to people without their permission, find out if they would prefer some other form of communication. Include a phone number where they can reach you.

Internet Discussion Forums

Networking is considered a very effective job search and career planning strategy. *Building and nurturing professional relationships are important to career health.* That's one of the major benefits of professional associations and clubs. But active membership usually requires time and travel. Furthermore, there may not be an organization that covers your interest in your local area. The Internet is an excellent networking tool. From the comfort of a personal computer, you can access people who share your interests. Newsgroups, message boards, e-mail groups, and chat rooms are all sources for Internet networking.

Neal is a gourmet chef and a member of the Minnesota Culinary Association. He is seldom able to make the association meetings because of his busy schedule. In order to stay current with culinary trends and to improve his management skills, he participates in newsgroups and e-mail discussion groups. Through these groups, he is able to connect with other chefs from all over the world. Neal has learned a lot from these groups which helped him improve his skills and performance. The result has been steady promotions and salary increases. Since Neal is an active participant in these groups (asking questions, responding to other participants, participating in discussions), he has built a small, but important, national reputation. As a result, many fine restaurants around the country have approached Neal to consider working for them.

Tips for Group Discussion:

- Keep your communication consistent with the intended group topic.
- Keep your response directed to the current subject.
- Don't change the subject in the middle of the thread.
- Don't add a new subject to an existing thread.
- If you want to start a new discussion, begin with a new subject.
- Consider when to respond to the group or to a specific individual.
- Respond to the individual if your reply is personal, not consistent with the group's topic, or if you want to limit the response.
- Respond to the group when your reply is of interest to the group.
- Find out if the group has published a FAQ (frequently asked questions) file and read it before participating in the discussion.
- Spend time lurking before you participate in a discussion.

Networking is considered a very effective job search and career planning strategy.

Internet Job Search Strategies

THE ELECTRONIC RESUME

The electronic resume is an important job search tool. It's a job seeker's advertisement of skills, qualifications and accomplishments. It is intended to attract the attention of potential employers and captivate them to meet with the job seeker. The resume is also a tool for inputting a job seeker's qualifications into a database to be searched and sorted by employers. The resume is an important tool in an effective Internet job search campaign.

Sending Your Resume by E-mail

The resume is a communication tool. Traditionally, the resume is sent to prospective employers by *snail mail* (U.S. Post Office), FAX, or is delivered in person. Today we can add e-mail to the list. E-mail is a very effective way to send someone your resume. It can be sent either as part of the body of the e-mail message, or as an attachment. The recipient can then print a paper copy of the resume, save an electronic copy, or import the resume into a database.

Tips for Distributing Your Resume by E-mail:

- Generally, it is best not to send an unsolicited resume (unsolicited resumes usually do not get read).
- Do not mass-mail your resume. Experts say that only two out of every 100 unsolicited resumes are read. Also, Internet users generally dislike unsolicited e-mail (spam).
- Include a cover letter message when sending a resume. Indicate in the message your intent to follow-up with the person.
- Send the resume to a specific person. Avoid sending the resume "To Whom it May Concern," or to a generic job title.
- Consider targeting your resume to the needs of the specific employer. This requires researching the employer and editing your resume prior to sending it.
- Follow-up by phone or e-mail on each resume you send.
- If you are concerned about the visual quality of your resume after it has been sent by e-mail, consider following-up by sending a paper copy.
- If you are sending your resume as an e-mail attachment, make sure the recipient can receive attachments.
- If you are sending your resume in a proprietary format such as Microsoft Word or WordPerfect, be sure the recipient has the correct version of the program so they can read your resume. If you are unsure, e-mail or call to confirm. Otherwise, send your resume in an ASCII format.

Posting Your Resume to a Database

Many employers manage and sort resumes in a resume database. They search the database for specific skills and qualifications. A well-written resume with the right skills and qualifications will show up frequently and prominently in the employer's search. It will capture the employer's attention and interest when reviewed. Effective resumes are those that contain many skill words, communicate motivation, and demonstrate performance. A poorly written resume, or one with limited qualifications, will not show up in an employer's search and will not be viewed.

Resume databases favor the most skilled candidates or those who have the most effective resumes. One advantage to the job seeker is that his/her resume will usually stay current in the database much longer than in a filing cabinet. If the resume does not show up in a search today, it has a chance of showing up in a search in the future.

There are several common ways that a resume is placed into a database. It may be entered directly, a paper resume may be scanned, or an electronic resume may be imported into the database. Any resume (paper or electronic) may find its way into a database. While the original format for the resume may vary, once it's in the database, it will usually be stored in an ASCII format.

CREATIVE Job Search

Internet Job Search Strategies

Posting Your Resume to Newsgroups

Newsgroups are another place where you can post your resume. Most newsgroups are discussion forums where people who share similar interests can exchange and browse messages. Many newsgroups with professional topics can be excellent places to meet people, but they are usually not a good place to post your resume. It would be like going to a local professional club or association meeting wearing a sign that says, "Help me, I'm looking for work." You would probably be avoided. But you may meet people through a newsgroup that you would want to send your resume to by e-mail. However, not all newsgroups are discussion forums. Many are set up for advertising items for sale, listing job openings, or for posting resumes. Many progressive recruiters look in these newsgroups for qualified candidates. It may be worth your effort to have your resume posted in select resume newsgroups. Resumes posted to newsgroups will nearly always be in an ASCII format.

Tips for Posting Resumes:

- Newsgroup postings are deleted or archived after a period of time. To keep your resume current it must be reposted periodically.
- Many resume databases also have a specific period that the resume is active. Check with the provider to learn how long the resume is active and how to extend the time. If the resume will stay active indefinitely, learn how to remove the resume when you no longer want it posted.
- Resume posting to newsgroups opens you up to spam (unsolicited e-mail). Be prepared to screen out the advertisements. Remember, if it sounds too good to be true, it probably is. Alternatives include using a fictitious e-mail address or not listing an address. However, this will also limit the ability for employers to contact you.
- If you are contacted from a posting, screen the person carefully before you give any additional information or schedule a meeting! Ask for a phone number where you can call them back. Find out if they have a website you can access.
- Don't be offended if a recruiter wants to network with you. They may be hoping you know someone with the qualifications that they desire. If they are a legitimate recruiter, it may lead to something for you.
- Don't give out the names of your friends or associates. If you want to make a referral, give the name of the employer to your friend to follow-up on.

Internet Job Search Strategies

Resume Content

The content of an electronic resume should follow the same wisdom used for producing a paper resume. Instead of just providing a list of where you worked and attended school, your resume should sell your qualifications. It should not only say what you can do, but should stress your performance and accomplishments. The resume should be skill-based and database friendly. Skills are important to employers. Skill words are important keywords when searching for resumes in a database. Many employers today use a resume database. Therefore, all resumes should be easily managed in a database.

While the content and use of an electronic resume follows the same wisdom as a paper resume, the formatting is very different. It is possible to distribute your resume through the Internet in a word processing file format such as Microsoft Word or WordPerfect. In its original format, it can be sent as an e-mail attachment or made available to download from a web page or newsgroup. However, it will only be available to people who have the program that matches the file format (i.e., Microsoft Word or WordPerfect). Also, any number of things can go wrong with the transfer. ASCII text is the preferred format for distributing your resume on the Internet.

Resume Content:

- Emphasize your skills.
- Include industry and employer specific keywords.
- Use contemporary language (i.e., keyboarding instead of typing).
- Stress your performance; use measurable outcomes and values.
- Target your qualifications to the needs of the employer.

Resume Formatting

ASCII is a code that allows computers to communicate. ASCII files are also called text files. The strength of ASCII is that all computers can read information in this format. The difficulty is that the only formatting options available are what can be accomplished with keystrokes on the keyboard. That eliminates **bold**, *italic*, underline, *fancy fonts*, large fonts, and word wrap. It also makes it more difficult to indent, center, right justify, or create lists. With a little creativity it is possible to create an attractive text resume.

ASCII Formatting Suggestions:
- Use capital letters for EMPHASIS, but not for the entire text.
- Use double returns to create white space.
- Use an asterisk (*) to bullet. Be sure to put a space between the asterisk and the text.
- Use spaces to indent.
- Insert hard returns at the end of each line. The resume may word wrap on the screen, but when you send or post it you may have lines that extend beyond the right margin.
- Use 66 characters for your line length to ensure that your resume stays formatted.

Your resume should sell your qualifications.

Sample Resume: ASCII Text Layout

RED E. JOBHUNTER
Phone: (555) 555-5555
e-mail: jobhunter@success.com

OBJECTIVE: Medical Laboratory Technician requiring extensive experience as a registered Medical Lab Technician with success in pediatrics and at a trauma emergency hospital.

SUMMARY OF SKILLS AND EXPERIENCE

LAB TECHNICIAN— Highly skilled lab technologist with experience serving ER, Urgent Care, Pediatric ER, and Stab-Room Trauma Unit. Processed cultures in microbiology, gram stains, urinalysis, and various manual tests.

PHLEBOTOMY— Inpatient and outpatient, pre-op and post-op, blood draws. Recognized for exceptional skill in serving hard to draw patients and children.

INSTRUMENT MAINTENANCE— Skilled in troubleshooting and maintenance of technical equipment.

TEACHING— Responsible for training staff on equipment operation and procedures.

QUALITY CONTROL— Maintained high quality standards with an emphasis on accuracy. Maximized lab performance through organization, equipment testing, and procedures development.

EMPLOYMENT HISTORY

MEDICAL LABORATORY TECHNICIAN, ASCP
May, 198_ to September 199_ Hennepin County Medical Center
* Increased lab efficiency through improved processing procedures, development of technical equipment, lab layout, and design.
* Maintained peak lab performance. Blood samples from Stab-Room Trauma Unit had to be accurately processed within two minutes!
* Assisted medical staff in the research and development of "Kiss of Life" mask used in respiratory emergency care.

PHLEBOTOMIST
August 198_ to March 198_ Minneapolis Children's Medical Center

---

EDUCATION

CERTIFIED: American Society of Clinical Pathologists
MEDICAL LABORATORY TECHNICIAN (GPA 3.5)
College of St. Catherine 198_
BIOLOGY / CHEMISTRY (117 credits)
Mankato State University 198_

HYPERTEXT RESUME

Many progressive job seekers are creating professional websites to promote themselves to potential employers. These hypertext resumes use the features of the World Wide Web. They may include graphics, video, sound, hypertext links, direct e-mail, and more. Additionally, some sites that post resumes require them to be formatted in Hypertext Markup Language (HTML). The cost to setup such a site is often reasonable. Many Internet service providers include space for a web page as part of their service package.

The hypertext resume should follow the publishing standards of the World Wide Web. They include effective layout and design as well as the use of frames, JAVA, plug-ins, animations, etc. There are many resources on the Internet, in bookstores, and in libraries to help you learn how to create a website. Most of the major word processing programs convert documents into HTML. There are also software products designed specifically for writing web pages. Information can be found on the Learn the Net Internet site:
www.learnthenet.com

The hypertext resume should follow the basic standards of resume writing (with a few exceptions). To learn more about writing resumes, contact your local Minnesota WorkForce Center, or check the *Creative Job Search* Internet site:

www.MnWorkForceCenter.org/cjs/cjs_site

How you use your resume is just as important as how it is written. Placing a resume on the Internet, hoping an employer will stumble on it is like leaving your paper resume laying around in public places as a job search strategy. Actively refer contacts to your web page. Include your Internet address in your paper cover letters, e-mail correspondence, and on personal business cards.

To view samples of personal web pages designed as a job search tool, go to your favorite search engine and search on the keyword "resume." You will find many samples to preview. Don't just look for people with the same experience and background you have. Consider how they have created a professional appearance using the tools of the web.

Tips for Hypertext Resumes:

- If you have a personal web page, keep it separate from your professional web page. Personal information does not belong in your job search.
- Use graphics sparingly and only those that enhance your professional image. Be sure your resume is readable and attractive, with the graphics "turned off."
- Unless you are a web developer or graphic designer, avoid animations and advanced web features.
- Consider making your site more than just your paper resume online. Include more detail about your qualifications, work samples, and accomplishments.
- A good website should be easy to navigate. The home page should capture readers' interest and allow them to choose what they would like to view.
- Do not post pictures of yourself on your professional web page. Personal pictures open up the opportunity for bias and discrimination.
- Pictures of professional accomplishments can provide excellent work samples. Keep the file size of graphics small, so they are easy to download.

How you use your resume is just as important as how it is written.

Internet Job Search Strategies

INTERNET EMPLOYMENT SERVICE PROVIDERS

One popular enterprise is the Internet employment service. These sites are an excellent source of job opportunities and information. The services these sites provide are similar. However the industries, geographic locations, and job seekers they serve can be quite different. Some serve all occupations and industries while others specialize. Some are national or international in their scope while others serve a limited geographic area. Some sites specialize in services for youth, recent college graduates, self-employment, minorities, women, and persons with disabilities.

Common Services

Job Posting— listings of job opportunities or employers seeking qualified applicants.
Resume Posting— job seekers post their resume to a database for employers to search.
Job Search Instruction— information on effective job search strategies.
Labor Market Information— information on occupations, wages, and employment.
Legal Information— information on hiring, discrimination, and personnel issues.
Training Information— information on training resources and financial assistance.

Advanced Services

Automated Screening of Jobs— the site automatically screens new jobs and sends the job seeker messages by e-mail announcing opportunities that meet their interests.
Automated Resume Distribution— the ability to send a resume on file with the site directly to employers listing job opportunities.
Resume Tracking— reports showing the activity of a resume listed in a database (i.e., number of times the resume has matched an employer's search and how many times the resume has been viewed).
Message Boards and Chat Rooms— discussion forums where job seekers can share ideas and ask questions about their job search.
Professional Advice— resume review and expert guidance from professional employment consultants through e-mail, chat rooms, and message boards.

Among the benefits of these sites are their convenience. Traditional employment services are offered in select locations. Internet employment services can be accessed from anywhere there is a computer connected to the Internet. In addition to home computers, this includes libraries, community centers, and Minnesota WorkForce Centers. Expect these sites to grow as the Internet continues to grow.

All job seekers should consider using these services. They are an excellent addition to a traditional job search. In Minnesota, check out the Minnesota Department of Economic Security Internet site:
www.MnWorkForceCenter.org
This site offers nearly all the services previously mentioned.

Internet Job Search Strategies

Minnesota's Job Bank

You can register to look for work by setting up an Internet account on Minnesota's Job Bank. Establishing an account and logging onto Minnesota's Job Bank will give you access to job openings, resume posting, career information, training opportunities, and information on all Minnesota WorkForce Center events and services.

Employers and private employment agencies will have access to your resume. They can view your qualifications in relationship to their job openings. If interested, employers will contact you directly.

There are step-by-step instructions for easy use of the system. You have the personal control of updating or removing your resume. Your resume will be done in an attractive and standardized format. There will also be other links to job-related websites for career and job search information, and other local services and information. There is no charge for this service. Hundreds of new jobs are posted every day, so be sure to check back often.

If you do not have Internet access, you can visit your local public library, school, university, a Minnesota WorkForce Center, or local employment service. Minnesota's Job Bank can be found on the Internet at **www.mnworks.org**

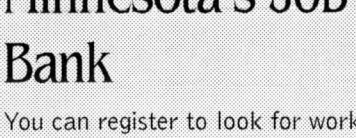

America's Career Kit

America's Job Bank
America's Job Bank (AJB) is a large national database of job openings. Relocate to other parts of the country by finding a job through AJB. You can search for jobs or create a "Scout" for any other state or territory in the U.S.

America's Career InfoNet
Visit this site before making important career decisions. You will find out more about the job market in every state. You will learn about employment trends and what kind of training you will need to qualify for jobs which interest you.

America's Learning eXchange
This site will help you find the training and education that is available to best prepare you for a new career or to upgrade your skills.

America's Career Kit can be found on the Internet at **www.ajb.dni.us**

Tips for using Internet employment services:

- Choose providers that best meet your occupational and geographic goals.
- Research the employer before applying for job opportunities.
- Follow-up on jobs for which you have applied.
- Use the services actively, not passively. Visit the site frequently. Follow-up quickly on job postings.
- Finally, don't invest the majority of your effort on these services. *Remember, the best job search strategies are still direct employer contact and networking.*

CREATIVE Job Search

Internet Job Search Strategies

Tips for Learning the Internet

Learn the Net site provides information and instruction for effectively using the Internet:

www.learnthenet.com

Spend time on the Internet: The only way to master the Internet is by using it. Plan to invest time and energy into learning the Internet. The Internet is constantly changing. To stay current you need to learn and relearn the Internet.

Manage your Internet time: Avoid marathons. Regular short periods of time are more effective than infrequent long periods. When you go on the Internet, decide in advance what you want to accomplish.

Read magazines, books, and web pages: Everything you need to know about the Internet can be found on the Internet. Excellent information about the Internet can also be found in books, magazines, and periodicals.

Attend classes or seminars: Seminars are useful for learning about the Internet. Hands-on classes are an excellent way to master Internet skills. Use the newly learned skills immediately and repeatedly.

Network: Talk about the Internet with associates, friends, and family. Participate in Internet newsgroups, chat rooms, and message boards. How much you learn by asking questions, listening, and sharing your knowledge with others may surprise you.

Look for opportunities to use the Internet: When you need information, see if you can find it on the Internet. Search for a phone number, address, map, or an item for sale in the newspaper. Research a hobby, a dream vacation, business, or professional topic. Explore different search strategies and search engines.

Challenge yourself: Look for new opportunities to use the Internet. Study a new website or learn another Internet resource.

Make the Internet a priority: Incorporate the Internet into your professional, social, and personal life.

Minnesota WorkForce Centers are available to help you with your job search. Resource areas in the WorkForce Centers offer computers with state of the art software for resume writing, career exploration, and job search. Professional staff are available to assist you with your efforts. To locate the Minnesota WorkForce Center near you, call 1.888.GETJOBS.

Minnesota WorkForce Centers and the Minnesota Department of Economic Security provide extensive employment resources on the Internet: **www.MnWorkForceCenter.org** These resources are available from any computer with Internet access.

The Internet is quickly becoming a basic part of how we receive information, communicate, and conduct business. It is also becoming an important tool in an effective job search campaign. People who learn to use the Internet will have a significant advantage over those who do not. It is worth taking the time to learn the Internet and use it as part of your job search.

NOTES

Internet Job Search Strategies

NOTES

The Job Interview

T he Interview is not the time to practice, it is the time to perform!

The Job Interview

Congratulations! All the hard work of your job search has just paid off. You have met the employer's minimum qualifications and captured her/his attention— you have been offered an interview. Now is the time to intensify your efforts. Preparation has been the force behind your job search, and further preparation is the key to a successful interview.

Congratulations! You have been offered an interview.

INTERVIEW PREPARATION

Knowing the kind of information the employer is likely to seek will help you prepare for the interview. Employers want to know your motivation for employment, your ability to do the job, how you will fit into the organization, and how much you will cost them. Being able to answer probing questions in these areas will make for a successful interview. While you already have some information about the employer, you may need to do further research in preparation for the interview.

It is to your advantage to know as much as you can about the job before that first interview. It will help you to target your skills to the specific needs of the employer and demonstrate your enthusiasm for the job. It shows that you are serious about employment.

Employers have limited information from which to make a decision: an application or resume, references, and a brief interview. It is up to you to convince the employer you are the best person for the job. All employers are looking for people who want to work. Most jobs require basic skills related to the specific job. For instance, a computer operator should know computer systems, an accountant understands accounting principles, and a welder must be proficient in welding applications. In order to have a successful interview, the computer operator needs to know the type of equipment and programs used. The accountant would want to find out which accounting system is used. The welder needs to know the different types of materials to be welded and the applications necessary to perform the welds.

Jack received a call from an employer regarding an accounting position. His efforts have paid off. They want to schedule an interview! While Jack is on the phone scheduling the interview, he takes advantage of the opportunity. He inquires about the responsibilities of the position and asks them to send a position description and corporate report. Preparing for the interview, Jack studies these documents. He finds additional information at the library and on the Internet. Jack writes down the skills and qualifications he believes the employer will be seeking. Then he considers how his qualifications match those needs. He is encouraged to discover that he meets eight out of the ten major requirements. For the two that are a weak match, Jack spends additional time preparing for how he will address his deficiency.

With the help of a friend, Jack set up a mock interview where he practiced answers to common interview questions. Jack takes with him his resume, the position description, the corporate report, a note pad, an outline of his research, and his resume references.

At the interview there are no surprises. Jack is relaxed and confident. He anticipated the needs of the organization and is prepared to answer each question, even questions in those areas where his qualifications are weak. Occasionally, he refers to the marked up position description, corporate report, and his notes. He offers his references at the end of the interview. Jack is on the path to success. He is doing all that he can to succeed and ultimately his efforts will pay off.

The Job Interview

Research Questions

Information about the employer can be obtained by talking with the person scheduling your interview. Ask about the interview process, who you will be interviewing with (one person or a panel), the length of time to plan to be there, directions, address and phone number, parking location, and if you are to bring anything other than your resume.

- If you need an accommodation due to a disability, let them know of your need.

- Ask for a written job description. This will be very helpful when trying to identify specific skills.

- Ask a current employee what personality traits are most useful when working for this employer.

- Who are the customers of this business? What products or services are offered to customers?

- What is the management philosophy?

The list goes on and on. The more you know, the better prepared you will be at the interview. Other sources of information include: employer brochures, annual business reports, trade periodicals, manufacturers' guides, union representatives, school placement offices, Minnesota WorkForce Centers, local employment service offices, Chambers of Commerce, and professional organizations.

See the chapter on Job Search Preparation to review information on researching employers.

Matching Skills

Once you have gathered as much information as possible, list the specific skills, experience, and employment attributes sought by the employer. Write down how your qualifications meet those requirements. If you are deficient in an area, you must be ready to convince the employer you can and will learn the skill. You could also show how other skills you have make up for this weakness. Having a plan of action to overcome the deficiency should impress the employer. For example, you lack skill in programming in C++ language. Knowing when and where you can enroll in a C++ course in your community may convince the employer you are the right person to hire.

Nancy wants a job in human services helping people. She has no paid work experience and recently completed her GED. However, she has answered phones for her uncle's business, coordinated mailings for her community center, did some fundraising for the Cancer Society, and volunteers at a food shelf. By matching the skills on her resume to those skills that the employer needs, Nancy was able to get a job as an information coordinator at a resource center.

The Job Interview

Attitude

Employers are looking for people with a positive work attitude. Often employers emphasize attitude over skills, training, and experience. Look for ways to show your enthusiasm for the job, willingness to learn, spirit of cooperation, and respect for the employer. Prepare yourself mentally with positive self-talk. Review your skills for reinforcement of your qualifications. Pay attention to what you are telling yourself before the interview: Is it positive, truthful, and realistic?

Appearance

A critical part of the impression you make on an employer is based on your physical appearance. An employer might reason that the person who doesn't care about her/his appearance will not care about the job. **Neat, clean, and conservative** is a safe standard for dress and grooming. Dress a step above what the best employee for that job would wear. Avoid excessive jewelry, perfumes, and colognes. Stay away from "fads" in clothing and shoes. **Look the part.**

Make a Good Personal Appearance:

- Get a good night's sleep
- Take a shower
- Shave
- Brush your teeth
- Use a mouthwash
- Comb your hair
- Wear clean and pressed clothes
- Wear proper clothes for the job
- Clean and shine your shoes
- Avoid smoking before the interview

Your personal appearance makes an immediate statement. If you were hiring someone for the position you are seeking, what would be important to you? What is your appearance saying?

Life is 10% what happens to you and 90% how you react to it!

Charles Swindoll

George was applying for a building maintenance job. He had no employment history in maintenance, but he had developed the skills needed by repairing his home. He was competing with others who had lots of experience. For the interview, he wore a new pair of overalls, a tool belt loaded down with tools, and displayed a positive attitude. He got the job!

The Job Interview

TYPES OF INTERVIEWS

The purpose of an interview is to get acquainted and to learn about one another. Employers evaluate your qualifications for the job. You help them with this evaluation by being prepared to sell your skills and experience. It is also an opportunity for you to evaluate the employer. As this learning process takes place, both parties develop expectations.

You may experience different kinds of interviews during your job search. It is important that you understand the purpose of each. Three very common types of interviews are: telephone screening, in-person screening, and the selection interview. No matter which type of interview, your goal is to present your qualifications to the final decision maker (the person who makes the decision to hire). Not everyone you come into contact with will be the decision maker. However, you should treat each person as though they have the authority to hire you (from the parking attendant, to the secretary, to the CEO).

Telephone Screening Interview

This interview saves the employer time by eliminating candidates based on essential criteria such as employment objective, education, or required skills. Since these interviews will often occur unexpectedly, it is important that your job search records are organized and kept where you can reach them at a moment's notice. This is a good reason to have a dedicated place in your home for your job search. Keep your resume in view and refer to it as needed.

In-Person Screening Interview

This interview is used to verify the candidate's qualifications for the position and to establish a preliminary impression of the candidate's attitude, interest, and professional "style." This interview is most often conducted by a professional screener from the employer's human resources department.

At this stage, the goal is to select candidates to meet with the decision maker.

Selection Interview

Conducted by the decision maker, the purpose of this interview is to probe the candidate's qualifications and to assess the "comfort level" with which the candidate might establish working relationships. There may be numerous interviews at this stage. As the number of candidates is "whittled down," you may be invited back to speak with the same person and/or with other managers or members of the work group. Your ability to establish rapport and present yourself as the right person for the position is critical.

Even if there is only one decision maker, the opinions of the others will be sought and will probably have an effect on the outcome. When you are invited to interview with a number of people, it is important that you present yourself effectively to each one of them. Remember, they will be evaluating your skills and ability to "fit in." As always, be yourself, but "sell" to each person's individual concerns.

Work Sample Interview

This interview is done to allow the applicant an opportunity to "show their wares." It could be the place for a graphic artist to display his/her portfolio. A salesperson may be asked to make a sales presentation. An office worker may be asked to complete a business letter using a specific type of computer software program.

The Job Interview

Peer Group Interview

This interview is an opportunity for you to meet and talk with your prospective co-workers. Just as in other interviews, the peer group will be evaluating you, determining how you "fit in."

Group Interview

Sometimes referred to as a panel interview, it usually consists of three or more people, all asking questions. Direct your answer to the individual asking the question, but try to maintain some eye contact with the other members of the group. Don't forget to smile. It shows confidence.

Luncheon Interview

"The Meal"— This type of interview assesses how well you can handle yourself in a social situation. Employer representatives may include the hiring manager, a human resource department member, and one or more peer employees. Choose your meal selection carefully. Spilling on your blouse or tie is not likely to make a favorable impression. Select healthy and easy things to eat so you can answer questions and pay attention to the conversation.

Stress Interview

A stress interview introduces you not to an interviewer, but to an interrogator. The interview is one in which you're treated as though you're the enemy. The "interrogator" asks you a number of offensive questions that are designed to deliberately make you uncomfortable. Keep your cool, take your time in responding to the questions, and when it is all over, reward yourself. Do not take it personally. This is usually a test of how you will handle stress on the job.

Video Conference Interview

Some employers today use video conferences to conduct meetings or carry out other aspects of their business. Conducting an interview via video conference enables an employer to save travel costs and still have, in effect, a "person-to-person" interview. If the thought of facing a camera during an interview frightens you, practice before a video camera or a mirror.

131 CREATIVE Job Search

The Job Interview

INTERVIEWING TIPS

Communicate Your Best Image By Being Prepared

- Dress **appropriately**: Select clothing appropriate to the job for which you are interviewing.

- Note business address, telephone number, and name of your interviewer.

- Arrive on time for the interview. Plan your schedule and route so you arrive 10 to 15 minutes prior to the appointment time. You may also want to consider driving to the address prior to the interview so you will know exactly where you need to be.

- Fill out applications neatly, completely, and in black ink. Be sure to bring your personal data sheet.

- Bring a notebook, black pen, your personal calling card, and extra copies of your resume.

- Bring letters of recommendation, your reference list, copies of licenses, driving record (for those jobs that require it), and social security or alien card.

- Also bring any other documentation supporting your qualifications (portfolio, work samples).

- Review questions you can ask in the interview.

- Review your resume and personal data sheet for related skills.

- Review answers to why you are the best person for the job.

Send Good Signals

- More than 50 percent of your communication is nonverbal. Your posture, walk, dress, facial movement, energy, gestures, and eye-contact are all nonverbal signals.

- Use a natural greeting, shake hands firmly, but only if a hand is offered to you first.

- Show reserved confidence. Let the interviewer start the dialogue. Listen carefully. Have good questions prepared **before** the interview.

- Ask thoughtful questions to find out if the employer's philosophy is compatible with yours. Discover if the job is right for you.

Communicate Attitudes

- You are willing to work. Give examples of your productivity on past jobs.

- Tell the employer about your skills. If you don't, no one else will! Don't make the employer work harder than you during the interview.

- You expect to make a contribution. Emphasize what you can do for the employer.

- You are flexible. Employers want employees who can adjust, work well with others, and fit into a new environment without complaints or special requests. Tell a story from your experience that illustrates your flexibility.

- You are committed to learning. Demonstrate this through examples of learning experiences (independent study, professional development, education, workshops, awards). Your plan for future development also communicates your commitment to learning.

Every interview is a learning experience. Use each interview as a building block for the next one. You may go through many interviews before you connect with the right job! It is not what happened at the last interview that is important, but what happens at this one!

The Job Interview

Handle Difficult Questions

- Welcome all questions with a smile.
- Give direct, honest answers. Take your time. Develop the answer in your head before you respond. If you don't understand a question, ask for it to be repeated or clarified. You don't have to rush, but don't be indecisive.
- Ask questions in return.
- Be prepared. Answering difficult questions that may reflect negatively on you can be answered by using the "sandwich model." This model has a positive statement followed by admitting the negative situation, and ending with another positive statement about what you have done to overcome the problem. Ending with a positive statement leaves a positive impression. Anticipate tough questions and practice interviewing beforehand.

Question: Why were you let go?

Answer: My skills are in engineering. My employer decided those skills were no longer needed. Therefore, I have taken some training and upgraded my skills (specify) to meet the qualifications for this type of job.

Question: It appears you haven't worked in the last five years.

Answer: I have been busy going to school full-time (specify), raising two children, and managing my home. I am now prepared and qualified for this job.

Question: It appears you have not worked for the past 10 years.

Answer: I was trained in machine operation while at a correctional facility. I am now married, have completed my GED, and am ready to work for you.

Finish Strong

- Take the initiative— demonstrate interest by asking when the position will be filled.
- Summarize why you are qualified. This is the time to state strengths and qualities you may have forgotten to emphasize earlier. Mention a particular accomplishment or activity that fits the job.
- **If you want the job, say so!**
- Don't overstay your time.
- Ask what the next step is in the hiring process. Will there be additional interviews? When will the hiring decision be made? When could you call back for the decision?
- Be pro-active in your follow-up. Schedule the next interview. Arrange to call the employer to learn their decision.

Follow-up

- Evaluate the interview. What went well in the interview? How can you improve?
- Record your follow-up plans. Write the date and time for your next contact with the employer. Be sure you follow through on these plans.
- Send thank you letters or notes within 24 hours to each person with whom you interviewed. For information on thank you letters and notes, see the chapter entitled Finishing Touches.

Preparing for the Interview

- Find out the parking availability and directions to the employer
- Note the business address and telephone number
- Note the name of the person you are to meet
- Bring a notebook, black pen, and tissues
- Review questions you can ask in the interview
- Bring your personal business card
- Bring your application or personal data sheet and letters of recommendation
- Bring money for gas, public transportation, telephone calls, and parking
- Bring your social security card and driver's license or state picture identification

133 CREATIVE Job Search

The Job Interview

KEY INTERVIEW QUESTIONS

Sample Interview Questions

1. **Tell me about yourself.**
   This is an open-ended question often asked to help "break the ice" in the interview. The important thing to remember is to keep the answer job-related.

2. **Why are you interested in working for this company?**
   This will show the employer that you have done your "homework." State the positive things you have learned about the company and how they fit with your career goals. This shows the employer that you cared enough about the interview to prepare for it.

3. **Tell me about your education.**
   Even though your resume includes this information, some employers like to have you expand on the subject. Mention your grade point average and good attendance record. Include all classes, seminars, workshops, and on-the-job training you have attended that support your job goals.

4. **Why have you chosen this particular field?**
   This is one way to discover your enthusiasm and dedication to your career.

5. **Describe your best/worst boss.**
   This could be a **trap**. Do not present a negative picture of any past employers. If given a choice, always talk about your best boss. If pressed to describe the worst boss, pick a work-related characteristic that can be stated in a positive way. For example, "I had a supervisor who was vague when issuing assignments. I learned to ask questions so that I knew what was expected."

6. **In a job, what interests you most/least?**
   This will give the employer another gauge for measuring how well you will fit the job opening.

7. **What is your major weakness? Always turn this into a positive!**
   State a weakness and turn it into a positive by showing how you overcame the weakness. "In the past, it has been difficult for me to accept criticism from my peers. However, I have learned to value and solicit this input and it has improved my job performance."

8. **Give an example of how you solved a problem in the past.**
   It is important to be able to show the process you go through when presented with a problem. State the problem and the steps you followed to reach the solution.

9. **What are your strengths?**
   This is the time to describe the skills you have identified that will most effectively "market" you as an employee.

10. **How do others describe you?**
    Another way for the employer to ask this would be, "How would you fit into this work group?" If you are not comfortable with this question before the interview, call some friends and/or ask people you have worked with how they would describe you.

11. **What do you consider the most important idea you contributed or your most noteworthy accomplishment in your last job?**
    Give examples of ways in which you saved the employer time, money, or developed an office procedure that improved efficiency.

12. **Where do you see yourself in three years?**
    Telling the interviewer, "In your job!" is not a good idea. Do indicate that you hope to acquire sufficient skills and knowledge within that time to make a positive contribution to the company.

All interview questions are really the same question:

Why are you the best person for the job?

CREATIVE Job Search

The Job Interview

13. **Think about something you consider a failure in your life, and tell me why you think it happened.**
    Failure implies error. Answers that point to a negative should conclude with a success. For example, "In my last job, I was given an assignment to coordinate all travel plans for an international conference. About halfway through the process, I realized I had not gathered enough information to help attendees make good travel and lodging decisions. I had to take time out to do the research which put me under a severe time crunch. I learned to do my research sooner. I haven't had the problem since."

    "I dropped out of school at age 17 to work for a fast-food employer. I later realized I couldn't make enough money to raise my family. I returned to school in the evenings and acquired clerical skills so I am now qualified to do this job."

14. **How do you think you will fit into this operation?**
    This is the time to express your interest in the job and knowledge of the employer. The more you know about the operation the easier this question will be to answer.

15. **If you were hired, what ideas/talents could you contribute to the position or our company?**
    This is another great opportunity for you to sell your skills. By giving examples of past accomplishments, the employer can visualize your contribution to her/his company.

16. **Give an example where you showed leadership and initiative.**
    Even if you haven't had the title of lead worker, supervisor, or manager, give examples of when you recognized a job needed to be done and you did it.

17. **Give an example of when you were able to contribute to a team project.**
    Unless you have lived in a total void, you have been part of a team. Team work is used in sales because both parties have to state their needs and expectations, then negotiate the sale. Families, community activities, and school all require team work.

18. **What have you done to develop or change in the last few years?**
    This shows a willingness to be challenged and to improve. Employers are looking for people who are willing to continue learning. Talk about formal and informal educational opportunities you have pursued. Mention books and periodicals you have read related to your field of interest.

19. **Do you have any questions for me?**
    By asking questions, you again show interest in the job. Listed on the next page are some questions you may want to ask at your interview.

Keep your answers brief and job-related. Focus on your skills.

Good Luck!

The Job Interview

Sample Questions to Ask in an Interview

- What are the responsibilities and accountabilities of this position?
- How well is the position defined? Can its duties be expanded?
- Would you describe an average day on this job?
- What is the history of the position? Why is it vacant?
- What aspects of this job would you like to see performed better?
- What are the key challenges or problems of this position?
- Where can I go from here, assuming that I meet/exceed the job responsibilities?
- How would you describe the ideal candidate?
- What are the employer's short- and long-range objectives?
- What are some outside influences that affect company growth?
- Where does the company excel? What are its limitations?
- When and how will I be evaluated? What are the performance standards?
- With whom would I be working? Who would be my supervisor? Who would I supervise?
- What is the department's environment like?
- When will you make the hiring decision? May I call you for the decision? When is a good time?

Some Reasons People Don't Get Hired

- Poor personal appearance
- Overly aggressive
- Inability to express information clearly
- Lack of interest and enthusiasm
- Lack of planning for career; no purpose or goal
- Nervousness, lack of confidence and poise
- Over-emphasis on money
- Unwillingness to start at the bottom
- Lack of tact and courtesy
- Lack of maturity
- Negative attitude about past employers
- No genuine interest in the employer or job
- No eye contact with the interviewer
- Application form is incomplete or sloppy
- No sense of humor
- Late for interview
- Failure to express appreciation for interviewer's time
- Failure to ask questions about the job
- Gives vague responses to questions
- Does not follow-up with thank you note or phone call

The Job Interview

"Be a Star"

Everyone has a story to tell, and everyone loves a story. Before your interview, follow the "star" method. When interviewing, bring up your "star" stories. Employers will remember you by your stories.

- Write short statements of what tasks you did and the results achieved. Be very specific.

- Use the fewest number of words, but make your points stand out.

- When possible, use numbers to measure the activity, benefits, or results.

- How significant and/or believable is your accomplishment from an objective point of view?

Follow the STAR method:
- S—Situation
- T—Task
- A—Action
- R—Results related to the job

Illustrate in an interview how you:

- Identified a problem
- Identified possible solutions
- Selected a solution
- Implemented a solution and what the positive outcome was

Be Prepared

WRITE OUT answers to questions!

Illustrate:
  Your strengths
  Your leadership
  Your ability to learn new things
  Your contributions to the organization
  Your creativity in solving problems
    and handling people

Practice

You should have at least two to four stories to tell an interviewer about yourself. Don't merely say you get along well with people, tell a story. People remember specific illustrations of skills, experience, and education. Make yours memorable. Stand out from the crowd. Make your stories relate to the skills the employer is seeking. Don't forget your sense of humor. **SMILE**.

The Job Interview

LEGAL RIGHTS

Questions asked in an interview should focus on your qualifications for the job. Although recent legislation helps ensure that you are not asked illegal questions, occasionally these questions come up on an application or in an interview. Human resources personnel are usually aware of what's legal and illegal. Others involved in the hiring process may not have the same awareness.

It is your right to withhold information unrelated to the job. However, research shows that refusing to answer questions may hurt your employment prospects. Think through possible illegal questions ahead of time and decide how you will handle them. If it does not bother you to answer a question, go ahead and answer it. If the question does bother you, be prepared to address it in a way which will not offend the interviewer. The key to effectively handling difficult questions is to prepare suitable answers well before the interview.

Listed below are examples of legal and discriminatory questions (in the State of Minnesota). For more information, contact your state's Department of Human Rights, Minnesota WorkForce Center, or your local employment service.

Legal Questions:

- Describe your education.
- What experience qualifies you for this job?
- Do you have licenses/certifications for this job?
- Are you willing to travel?
- What name(s) are your work records under?
- Are you available for overtime?
- Do you have the legal right to work in the United States?

Discriminatory or Illegal Questions:

- What is or was your spouse's name or line of work?
- Have you ever filed a Workers' Compensation claim or been injured on the job?
- Do you have any physical impairments which would prevent you from performing the job for which you are applying?

Title I of ADA lists these additional prohibited questions:

- What is your hair/eye color? What is your height/weight?
- Have you ever been hospitalized? If so, for what condition?
- Have you ever been treated by a psychiatrist or psychologist? If so, for what condition?
- Is there any health-related reason you may not be able to perform the job for which you are applying?
- How many days were you absent from work because of illness last year?
- Are you taking any prescribed drugs?
- Have you ever been treated for drug addiction or alcoholism?

After a job offer has been made:

Employers may request:
- Birth certificate
- Affirmative action statistics
- Marital status
- Proof of citizenship
- Photographs
- Physical exam and drug testing
- Social Security card or alien registration card

The Job Interview

NOTES

The Job Interview

NOTES

Finishing Touches

9

By adding the finishing touches, you will be the most outstanding candidate and the best person to hire.

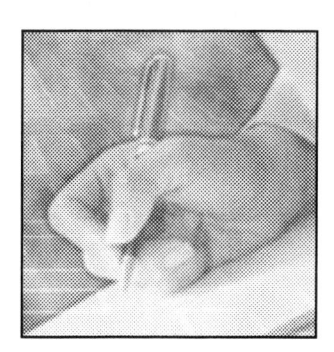

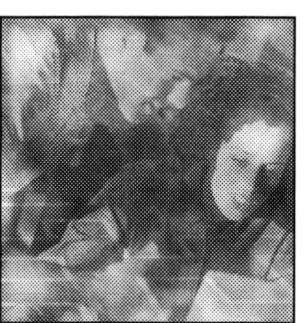

Finishing Touches

Now that your interview is over you can relax and wait for their answer— WRONG! In any good sales campaign, you have a plan, and you keep on selling. No interview is over until you have assessed the interview and written and mailed the thank you notes to all who interviewed you. You should also notify your references that they may soon be getting a telephone call from your prospective employer. Be sure to coach them on what you would like them to emphasize.

These are the extra steps that go into making you the outstanding and memorable candidate in the mind of the employer. If done correctly, these steps can put you a cut above the competition. Always think in these terms: "What is generally done by the typical job seeker?" "What else can I do to convince them I am the best person for the job?" This attitude will carry you through successful negotiation, gain on-the-job recognition, and foster career mobility. Do not be afraid to show you are the best person for the job by taking the initiative to do the extraordinary. By adding the finishing touches, you will be the most outstanding candidate and the best person to hire.

THANK YOU LETTERS AND NOTES

Saying "thank you" in your job search is not only the right thing to do, but is also an effective job search strategy. Every "thank you" is an opportunity to sell your qualifications and leave a positive impression on the reader. In your job search you should express your gratitude. Don't wait for opportunities— create them. Send a thank you letter or note to employers, employment contacts, and references whenever they have extended themselves. This includes after a job or informational interview, when someone gives you a referral or information, or whenever someone takes time out of their schedule to help you. Every person who assists you in your job search effort deserves an expression or note of thanks. Ask your references to keep you informed of contacts. Keep references informed about those employers/positions you are really interested in.

"Thank you" may be said in person, by phone, in a formal letter, or in an informal note. The best approach will depend upon the circumstances, personal style, and preference. The best strategy is to select the approach that best serves the immediate need.

Thank you letters and notes should be standard tools in your job search. The thank you letter should follow a standard business letter format, while the note may be a simple, handwritten note or card. The situation and your personal style will determine which you send.

At the minimum, a written thank you letter or note should be sent after all interviews. This is your opportunity to make one more impression before the decision is made. Send a written thank you letter even if you are turned down for a job. Let employers know that you appreciate their consideration, and you would be interested in future opportunities.

Thank you is a powerful statement. Unfortunately, it is seldom heard.

Finishing Touches

Points to Consider

- Write a thank you letter or note no later than 24 hours after the interview, even if things didn't go well.

- Be brief and to the point. Note the job you interviewed for, and also list the date of your interview.

- Always address a thank you letter to a person by name and title. Include your personal calling card if you have one.

- If there are multiple people, such as a panel interview, send a separate thank you to each person, or send a single thank you to a key person for distribution. When sending more than one thank you letter, it is very effective to vary each letter.

- When thanking a potential employer, restate your interest in the position and the employer.

- The thank you letter is an opportunity to again sell your qualifications. Briefly include any pertinent information you failed to mention earlier. Be sure to re-emphasize your most important qualifications and skills for the job. Note anything that was mentioned in the interview that you can enhance or you feel may not have been discussed fully.

- Offer to come in for another interview or to provide more information if needed.

- Always plan your follow-up. Make it a point to tell the person when and how you will be following through.

- Learn to say "thank you" when you are with the individual. Do not let that be all you do; follow-up with a thank you letter, note, or phone call. You may want to make the effort to meet with the person again for the primary purpose of saying "thank you."

- Of course, you should always say "thank you" whenever you are on the phone and someone helps you. There may be occasions when you would call someone specifically to thank them.

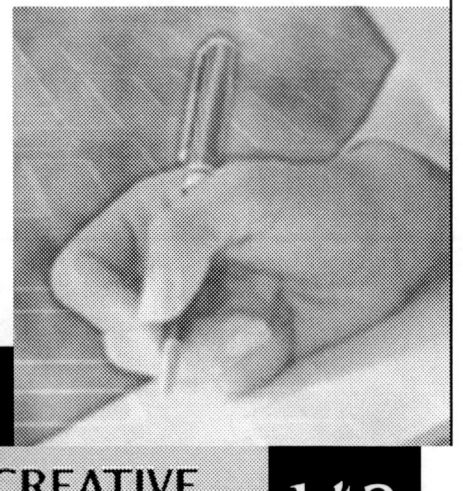

Finishing Touches

Sample Thank You Letter

2233 First Street
Anytown, MN 55555
(555) 555-5555

September 20, 200_

Mr. James Business
Human Resource Manager
ABC Company
111 Employment Way
Anytown, MN 55555

Dear Mr. Business:

Thank you for the opportunity this morning to discuss the secretarial position. Our conversation gave me a better understanding of ABC Company and the requirements of the job. The additional information from Max and Katherine was helpful in gaining a better perspective of the position.

My strong office and interpersonal skills will definitely make a contribution to your company. I am proficient in all the computer software packages you use, and I feel I possess the customer service experience you want.

I enjoyed meeting the office staff and touring the facility. This is clearly a quality organization with an emphasis on efficiency and a dedication to teamwork. I would consider it a privilege to join your team. I will contact you next week to inquire about the hiring decision.

Again, thank you for your time and consideration.

Sincerely,

Amy Applicant

Finishing Touches

Basic Parts of a Thank You Note

1. Statement of appreciation
2. Expressions of interest in the job
3. Brief restatement of qualifications/skills
4. An opportunity to add additional information you failed to mention
5. Final "thank you"
6. Date and time you will follow-up as previously agreed

Thank You
Thank You
Thank You
Thank You

Say it often . . .
Say it with style!

Finishing Touches

Sample Thank You Notes

February 29, 200_

Dear Ms. Smith,

Thank you for taking the time to discuss the accounting position with me. It was a pleasure meeting you and Mr. Jones. Lord's Industries sounds like the perfect place for me to use my skills, especially since you use the WXY system, the same system I have been supporting the past three years. My proven track record and accomplishments with cost-effective systems can be an asset to your company.

Again, thank you for your consideration. I will contact you by Tuesday of next week to learn of your decision. I look forward to the possibility of joining your staff.

Sincerely,

---

*February 29, 200_*

Dear Mr. Jones,

Thank you for the interview for the accountant position today. I appreciate the information you shared with me and enjoyed meeting Ms. Smith from the Accounting Department.

My interest in working for Lord's Industries is stronger than ever and, based on your description of the position, I know I can do a good job for you.

I will contact you by Tuesday of next week to learn of your decision.

Sincerely,

Thank you notes, whether handwritten or printed, must be clear, concise, and legible.

Finishing Touches

NEGOTIATING TIPS

This is a very important part of the job search process. It can set the tone for your work life and experience with the employer. These are some suggestions to consider when you receive a job offer. Negotiating is a two-way street. Try to achieve a win-win situation. It is up to you to decide the tips that will work best for you.

1. Know the salary you can reasonably accept and expect for the type of position you seek in comparison with your experience, education, and the industry wage standards.

2. Try and find out the salary range for the position before the interview. Contacting the interviewer's secretary, the personnel office, or a networking contact that works in the company may be helpful.

3. It is not usually recommended to accept an offer on the spot. Express your appreciation and strong interest in the job. Request at least 24 hours to consider it, even when saying "Yes." Ask any questions you need clarified.

4. Assess the job offer in terms of your needs, benefits, and long-term career and life goals. Talk it over with someone you respect. Make a list of the pros and cons of the job offer.

5. Consider if the job description is clear. Note your reporting relationships, authority, and advancement potential. Keep asking questions until it is clearly understood. Careful thought and consideration will only gain you respect.

6. If you want the job, make it clear this is the job you want. If you are uncertain, state there are some items you would like to discuss before you can accept the job. Suggest meeting further to talk about the offer.

7. Begin the negotiation with reasonable requests. Those requests could include more money, benefits, tuition, training, more vacation time, a flexible schedule, stock options, company car, on-site daycare, parking privileges, etc.

8. Negotiations should never become emotional or hostile. Use your value, skills, experience, and education to negotiate. Do not use your need for the job to negotiate.

9. Listen carefully. If the offer is less than you expected, let them know that, but state you are still interested in the position if they want to reconsider their offer. Don't assume the first offer is fixed. Even if the interviewer tells you it is— it rarely is.

10. If the same figure is offered a couple days later, it probably is the last offer. In that case, you can ask for a salary review in six months to evaluate your performance and value, or you can turn the job down, asking that they keep you in mind for future openings paying more money.

11. Even when saying "no," leave the door open to negotiation. (Do not use this to negotiate a higher wage. When you say "no," be ready to lose the job forever.)

12. When you reach an agreement, request the agreement in writing.

Finishing Touches

What to Do If You Get Turned Down

- Let interviewers know that although you are disappointed, you are still interested in working for the employer.

- Be sure to thank them for their time and interest. Re-emphasize the fact that if future openings occur, you would be interested.

- Find out if there are, or might be, other openings they could suggest or other persons you could contact.

- Many times the person selected ends up turning the job down or does not work out. Keep the communication line open, positive, and professional. This keeps your name in their mind for the next opening or future opportunities.

- Ask if you could contact them every three or four months to find out about future job openings.

- Stay positive. Congratulate yourself. You did get the interview, which means the employer was interested in you. Use positive self-talk (see Affirmations on page 18).

- Learn from the experience. Ask for feedback from the interviewer on what you could improve or do differently.

- Keep trying. This is not the time to stop. Forge ahead. Act to stay in control of your job search.

- Remember the salesperson's motto: "No" is another step closer to "Yes."

- Do not despair. Getting turned down happens to all of us at some point in our lives.

Finishing Touches

JOB SUCCESS SKILLS

Once you have made the big transition from job searching to landing the job, the next goal is job success. There are specific skills you need to know and use to be successful at your job. It is important to practice these skills prior to starting the job. First impressions show from day one. You only get one first impression.

This is not a complete list. It is a good idea to check with your supervisor about what is most important. Employers say more people lose their job because they do not use good work habits, rather than because they are not able to do the job. The following list of suggestions is based on feedback from a majority of surveyed employers.

Employer Expectations

- **A positive attitude** is one of the most important factors in achieving job success. Do not carry negative feelings into your new workplace; resolve them elsewhere.

- **Always be on time.** How long will it take to get to work? Allow a few extra minutes for traffic problems and getting children to day care. Set an alarm clock to help you get up. Being reliable and dependable gains the trust and respect of your new employer.

- **Good attendance and promptness** are always important. If you are going to be unavoidably late or out sick, ask your supervisor the proper method to notify them.

- **Know and follow** all office rules, policies, and procedures. Read the employee manuals.

- **Listen and learn.** Be open to new ways of doing things, even if you were taught differently in school or on a different job. Do not be quick to find fault, criticize, or complain until you can prove you can do something a better way.

- **Meet and exceed** your employer's expectations.

- **Learn all you can about the job** you were hired to do before thinking about moving up.

Communication

- **When you need to talk** with your supervisor, ask when would be a good time to meet.

- **Take advantage of your performance reviews.** Stay calm. Learn from them. Ask how you can improve. Show job-related classes you have taken. Most supervisors appreciate employees who are concerned about performance and finding ways to improve. Your job success is also their success.

- **Be a team player.** Be willing to help. Know the goals of your job and how your job fits into the overall organization. Avoid a "know-it-all attitude." Try to fit in with the team. Keep your sense of humor.

- **Ask for help** when you need it. If you make a mistake, let your supervisor know immediately. Find out how you can fix it.

- **Follow the proper chain of command.** Discuss items with your supervisor first.

Finishing Touches

Personal

- **Prior to starting the job**, have all of your appointments with doctors, dentists, etc., out of the way. Have your transportation and day care lined up so you do not immediately have to take time off. Have an emergency plan for day care and transportation.

- **Be willing to learn new skills.** Keep a record of classes you are taking that relate to the job. Review this with your supervisor at an appropriate time.

- **Take time in making new friends.** Find positive and upbeat co-workers. Avoid negative, critical, and gossiping people.

- **Be clean and well-groomed.** Wear clean and job-appropriate clothes. Pay attention to how your co-workers are dressed. Avoid wearing strong perfumes or colognes.

- **Keep your personal life and problems at home.** Do not use the employer's equipment and time to do personal things like making personal phone calls, using the copy machine, or resolving your personal problems on the job. If you are having trouble resolving personal problems, counseling, support groups, or employee assistance programs may be useful.

- **Create the image.** Dress for the job you want next.

- **Be patient with yourself and your employer.** It takes time to get used to, learn, and like a new job.

- **Volunteer for projects and committees** if your work is completed and your supervisor approves.

Getting Along With Others

- **Do not express your opinions, biases, or prejudices** about others while you are at work. Diversity is a priority in the workplace.

- **Accept criticism** as constructive. Do not become defensive or take criticism personally. Thank people for their input. Consider changing if it is warranted. If you are unsure how to handle the situation, check with your supervisor.

- **Always be friendly** to everyone. Be willing to go the extra mile. This creates goodwill with employers, co-workers, and customers.

- **Notice who your boss relies on** and model yourself after them.

- **Find a mentor**, someone who knows the employer and the job well enough to coach you or show you the ropes.

- **Realize playing politics or power games** could be dangerous and backfire on you.

- **Treat everyone with courtesy and respect.** Remember, as you climb the career ladder, you may meet the same people on your way down the ladder.

- **Keep your emotions under control.** The job is not the place to let your feelings get out of control.

- **Show appreciation.** Let your supervisor know you appreciate their training, support, input, feedback, etc.

- **Strive to be positively recognized.** Be friendly and helpful to everyone at all levels.

Finishing Touches

CONCLUSION

In today's world, job search is not usually a one-time event in most people's work life. Studies show that the average person will change jobs more frequently than in the past. People used to believe once they had secured a job with good pay and benefits, they would stay 20-30 years to retirement. Generally, this is no longer true for most people. The change is due, in part, to the fluctuating economy and fast-paced technological and scientific advances. That is why it is so important to learn the techniques of job search and consider it an invaluable and evolving life-time skill for present and future use. Job search skills need to be constantly maintained and updated throughout your work life— even when you are employed.

A recent case study has shown that once you have acquired these job seeking skill:

- Your confidence increases and your fears about looking for a new job are reduced.
- Your ability to interview and present yourself and your skills improves.
- You have more knowledge and are better prepared to move up the career ladder.
- You are considered more employable by potential employers when you are employed.
- You know more about the needs and trends of the labor market.
- You are more aware of your value and worth to your employer and the labor market.
- You gain freedom and independence from government programs.
- You know how to highlight your skills and abilities to stay ahead of the competition, achieve upward mobility, and negotiate successfully.

In order to make the most of the valuable skills and assets acquired through your job search training, it is recommended that you:

- Keep your skills current. Keep a list of new things you learn on the job and elsewhere.
- Update your resume when you have gained new skills, abilities, and accomplishments.
- Keep your options open. See what your job skills are worth in the job market. Go on interviews occasionally. Find out what you need to get to your goal, or what your marketable skills are worth. Expand your job by using all your skills.
- Get the training or experience you will need to move up or out.
- Keep a list of awards, accomplishments, and recognitions to present to your supervisor to lobby for a raise or for upward mobility. Also include that information on resumes and cover letters. Remember that you are your own best sales representative. It is up to you to manage, maintain, improve, and present your product— **you** and **your skills**.

Best wishes for your present and future success!

Finishing Touches

NOTES

Finishing Touches

NOTES